GERMAN REPORT SERIES

PECULIARITIES OF RUSSIAN WARFARE

REVISIED EDITION

DEPARTMENT OF THE ARMY
HISTORICAL DIVISION

Published by Books Express Publishing
Copyright © Books Express, 2011
ISBN 978-1-78039-062-8

Books Express publications are available from all good retail and online booksellers. For publishing proposals and direct ordering please contact us at: info@books-express.com

PECULIARITIES OF RUSSIAN WARFARE

PECULIARITIES OF RUSSIAN WARFARE

Preface

MS # T-22 was prepared by a committee of former German generals and general staff corps officers at the EUCOM Historical Division Interrogation Enclosure, Neustadt, Germany, in late 1947 and early 1948. The names of the committee members are not being announced at this time. All members, however, had extensive experience on the Eastern Front during the period 1941-45. The principal author, for example, commanded, in succession, a panzer division, a corps, a panzer army, and an army group.

The initial distribution of this report in early autumn 1948 was a severely limited one, including only those addressees to whom the report seemed to be of immediate, active concern. At that time, user agencies were cautioned that the report should not be used for purposes more precise than general background reading, because it contained certain errors of translation and of military terminology. During the intervening months, sufficient interest in the report has been evidenced to justify the preparation and distribution of a revised edition, on a much larger scale than was the case with the 1948 edition.

In the preparation of this revised edition, the German text has been retranslated, and ambiguities either resolved or called to the reader's attention when no other alternative was feasible. Certain changes in typography and in chapter and section titles have been made to improve clarity and facilitate use of the report by staff divisions and schools. All appendices have been redrawn and amplified, and a general reference map has been added to assist the reader in locating the various illustrative actions in the great expanse of the East.

The revised edition, therefore, is considered to be just as reliable and as sound as the text prepared by the German committee. The authors' prejudices and defects, whatever they may be, find the same expression in the following translation as they do in the original German.

HISTORICAL DIVISION
SPECIAL STAFF, U.S. ARMY
June 1949

PECULIARITIES OF RUSSIAN WARFARE

TABLE OF CONTENTS

	Page
FOREWORD	1
INTRODUCTION	2
THE RUSSIAN SOLDIER AND RUSSIAN CONDUCT OF BATTLE	4
PECULIARITIES OF RUSSIAN TACTICS	60
THE RED AIR FORCE	160
PARTISAN WARFARE	178
CONCLUSIONS	198

APPENDICES

PECULIARITIES OF RUSSIAN WARFARE

EXAMPLES

No.		Page

-1941-

No.		Page
1	Behavior of Russian Infantry near Bryansk and in the Citadel of Brest-Litovsk.	10
2	The Attempt to Starve Out an Encircled Russian Regiment on the Volkhov.	11
3	The Timoshenko War Game of February 1941.	17
4	General Petrov as Commander of Army Group Bryansk	19
5	A Commissar's Recommendations Concerning the Prohibition of Liquor	26
6	Liquidation of a Russian Company Commander by a Commissar	27
7	Russian Women in Combat (1941-42-43).	30
8	The Engagement at Maloryta (End of June 1941)	66
9	The Action Southeast of Plavskoye (November 1941)	67
12	Winter the Preferred Season for Russian Offensives (1941-45)	71
13	The Battle in the Dnepr---Beresina Triangle (Mid-July to Mid-August 1941)	73
14	Fighting in the Poretsye Bridgehead on the Luga (Mid-July to August 1941).	75
15	The Meeting Engagement near Plavskoye (November 1941)	77
16	The Tank Battle at Raseiniai (June 1941).	87

17	Russian Armored Counterattack near Rawa Ruska, Galicia	89
18	The Thrust on Vyazma (Early October 1941)	89
22	The Russian Defensive Effort during the German Break-Through of the Leningrad Line in the Fortified Krasnogvardeysk Region (September 1941)	109
28	Russian Defense in Woods during the Forward Thrust from the Poretsye Bridgehead on the Luga (August 1941)	136
31	A Siberian Rifle Division Breaks Through the German Lines at Uzlovaya under cover of Darkness (November 1941)	141
32	Night Break-Out of Encircled Troops	143
36	Atrocities as a Medium of Propaganda (1941-43)	154

-1942-

7	Russian Women in Combat (1941-42-43)	30
12	Winter the Preferred Season for Russian Offensives (1941-45)	71
19	Russian Tank Thrust on Kamenka and Millerovo (Winter 1942-43)	91
24	The Russian Defense against the German Relief Thrust on Stalingrad (December 1942)	118
27	The Russian Ambush of a German Battalion near Sukhinichi (February 1942)	135
33	Failures of Russian Defense in Night Operations (1942-43)	144
36	Atrocities as a Medium of Propaganda (1941-43)	154
38	Protection of Supply Lines near Kirovograd against Partisan Raids (1942-43)	194

-1943-

7	Russian Women in Combat (1941-42-43)	30
11	Russian Children as Intelligence Agents	70
12	Winter the Preferred Season for Russian Offensives (1941-45)	71
19	Russian Tank Thrust on Kamenka and Millerovo (Winter 1942-43)	91
20	The Tank Battle at Kharkov (August 1943)	92
21	The Break-Through in the Dnepr Bend south of Dnepropetrovsk (1943-44)	97
23	The Russian Defense System during the Pincers Attack on Kursk (July 1943)	116
26	Forest Fighting during the Russian Break-Through Attempt across the Upper Donets (August 1943)	132
30	Naked Russian Infantrymen Cross a Lake under cover of Darkness and Launch an Attack (September 1943)	140
33	Failures of Russian Defense in Night Operations (1942-43)	144
35	Deception by Individuals (1943-44)	150
36	Atrocities as a Medium of Propaganda (1941-43)	154
37	Desertion of an Uzbek Company (Byelgorod, 1943)	157
38	Protection of Supply Lines near Kirovograd against Partisan Raids (1942-43)	194

-1944-

10	Stationary Security Detachments as Protection for a Flanking Movement (Kandalaksha Front)	68
12	Winter the Preferred Season for Russian Offensives (1941-45)	71
21	The Break-Through in the Dnepr Bend south of Dnepropetrovsk (1943-44)	97
25	Break-Through of a Russian Tank Corps through Trackless Woodlands East of Lwow (June 1944)	131
29	Russian Thrust through the Pripyat Marshes toward Kowel (February 1944)	140
34	Successful Concealment of the First Russian Tank Army at Vinitsa (January 1944)	148
35	Deception by Individuals (1943-44)	150

-1945-

12 Winter the Preferred Season for Russian Offensives
(1941-45) 71

-x-

FOREWORD

1. The only written material available for the preparation of the following report consisted of a few memoranda in diary form, and similar notes of a personal nature. The report, therefore, is based to a preponderant degree on recollections of the author, and on material furnished by a small group of contributing commanders who had special experience in the East. For that very reason, it cannot lay claim to completeness. Moreover, the limited amount of time available to the author did not permit exhaustive treatment of the subject.

2. For the above-mentioned reasons, the report has had to be limited to a description of the characteristic traits of the Russian soldier, and their influence on the conduct of battle. The extent to which the political, economic, and social conditions of the country were influential factors, could only be touched upon. Orientation concerning climate and terrain--indispensable to an understanding of the Russian methods of warfare--has been omitted intentionally, since pertinent points on those subjects are discussed in MSS # T-34 and T-36.

3. In order to make the peculiarities of Russian warfare more comprehensible, numerous examples, varying according to place, time, and nature, are incorporated in this study. From these examples, conclusions can be drawn concerning not only Russian behavior, but also German countermeasures and experiences.

INTRODUCTION

4. The topics of Russian fighting strength and methods of warfare have more and more become matters of vital concern because of the surprisingly rapid developments in world politics. They have become subjects of public interest, perhaps even the issues that might decide the fate of Europe. Propaganda, legend, and politics already have obscured facts and reality. The most nearly correct appraisal will be arrived at by knowing the peculiarities of the Russian territory and its inhabitants, and by analyzing and accurately evaluating the sources from which they derive their strength. There is no better method than a study of World War II, the struggle in which the characteristics of country and people were thrown into bold relief, and in which they developed to the fullest all their latent vigor. Although the passage of time may meanwhile have diminished the value of these experiences, they nevertheless remain the soundest basis for an evaluation. The war potential* of the Soviet Union may be subject to change;

---
*Ed: Underscoring here, and in the subsequent paragraphs, is that of the author.

---

no doubt it has increased during the last few years and will increase further, at least until the end of the current Five Year Plan. The very latest implements of war surely have been further developed and produced in quantity, new offensive and defensive weapons perfected, and the main strategic emphasis shifted to the air force. Technological advances will alter the external aspects of warfare. But the character and peculiarities of the Russian soldier, and his particular methods of fighting, remain unaffected by the innovations. Nor will the characteristics of Russian topography change during the next few years. In these decisively important aspects, therefore, the conclusions drawn from the late World War remain fully valid.

5. Nevertheless, it is not easy to draw the correct conclusions from the experiences gained, because the means available to the opposing forces were very unevenly matched. Except for the first few months of the Eastern Campaign, we were, so to speak, constantly waging a war of the poor against the rich. Several Russian surprise attacks would have been detected in the assembly stage, had we but had sufficient reconnaissance facilities at our disposal. The Russians would not have broken through many a German position, had it been more adequately manned, and had sufficient materiel for defense been available. The danger exists, therefore, that Russian feats may be somewhat overrated.

6. On the other hand, that danger is lessened to a certain extent by the probability that also in the future any power waging war against the Russians will, so far as numerical strength is concerned, be in a position similar to ours in World War II. For that reason, it should be no grave error to generalize from the observations made in the East between 1941 and 1945.

THE RUSSIAN SOLDIER

AND

RUSSIAN CONDUCT OF BATTLE

MS # T-22

CONTENTS

	Page
Chapter One – PECULIARITIES OF THE RUSSIAN SOLDIER	6
Chapter Two – THE RUSSIAN COMMAND ECHELONS	15
Chapter Three – THE COMMISSAR	25
Chapter Four – THE COMBAT ARMS	32
I. Infantry	32
II. Artillery	36
III. Armored Force	39
IV. Horse Cavalry	41
Chapter Five – RUSSIAN COMBAT METHODS	44
Chapter Six – RUSSIA AS A THEATER OF OPERATIONS	55

Chapter One

PECULIARITIES OF THE RUSSIAN SOLDIER

7. No one who belongs to the Western sphere of culture will ever be able to understand the Russian completely, or to analyze the character and soul of this <u>Asiatic</u> who has grown up on the far side of the border of Europe. The Russian is <u>unfathomable</u>. He swings from one extreme to the other without our being able to recognize the reasons for his behavior. It is possible to predict from experience how practically every other soldier in the world will behave in a given situation--but never the Russian. The characteristics of the Russian soldier, like his vast country, are strange and <u>full of contradictions</u>. There were units which one day repulsed a strong German attack with exemplary bravery, and on the next folded up completely. There were others which one day lost their nerve when the first shells exploded, and on the next allowed themselves, man by man, literally to be cut to pieces. The Russian is generally impervious to crises, but he can also be very sensitive to them. He has no fear of a threat to his flanks, but at the same time he can be most touchy about the flanks. He disregards all the old established rules of tactics, but he clings to the absolute letter of his own precepts.

8. The key to this odd behavior can be found in the character of the Russian soldier, who, as a fighter, possesses neither the perception nor the ability to think independently. He is subject to

moods which for us are incomprehensible; he acts <u>instinctively</u>. As a soldier, the Russian is primitive and unassuming, brave by virtue of natural inclination, but morosely vegetating in a group. These characteristics make the Russian in many respects an adversary superior to the self-confident and demanding soldiers of other armies. The later can, and must, by their physical and mental qualities, achieve not merely equality, but superiority, so that they may stand up successfully against the Russian soldier.

9. <u>Disregard for human beings and contempt of death</u> are other characteristics of the Russian soldier that are incomprehensible to us in such a degree. The Russian soldier climbs with complete indifference and cold-bloodedness over the bodies of hundreds of fallen comrades, in order to take up the attack on the same spot. With the same apathy he works all day long burying his dead comrades after the battle. He looks toward his own death with the same resignation. Even severe wounds impress him comparatively little. For instance, a Russian who was sitting upright at the side of the street, in spite of the fact that both his lower legs were shot away, asked with a friendly smile for a cigarette. The Russian soldier endures cold and heat, hunger and thirst, dampness and mud, sickness and vermin, with the same <u>equanimity</u>. With his simple and primitive nature, all sorts of hardships cause but few reflexes within his soul. His emotions run the gamut from animal ferocity to the utmost kindliness; odious and cruel in a group, he is friendly and ready to help as an individual.

10. There can be no doubt that the sum of these most di-

verse characteristics makes the Russian a superior soldier, who, under the direction of an understanding leader, becomes a dangerous opponent. It would be a serious error to underestimate the Russian soldier, even though he does not quite fit into the picture of modern warfare and up-to-date fighters. The strength of the Western soldier is conscious action, controlled by his own mind, which accomplishes wonders. This acting on his own, the consciousness which accompanies the impulse, is not to be found in the Russian. But the fact must not be ignored that a <u>change</u> is taking place also in this respect. Even the difference between the Russian units in World War I and those in World War II was considerable. Whereas in the earlier war we faced a more or less amorphous mass, immovable and without countenance, the <u>spiritual awakening</u> through Communism made itself clearly felt in the last war. The number of illiterates was small, very much in contrast to the situation at the time of World War I. The Russian masses have acquired a countenance, or at least are well on the way to acquiring one. The Russian is beginning to become a conscious human being, and hence a soldier who is able to stand on his own feet. The number of good noncommissioned officers is still not large, and the Russian masses have yet to overcome their sluggishness, but their awakening is no longer far off. Whether this will work to the advantage or disadvantage of their soldierly qualities cannot yet be determined. Along with awareness flourish criticism and obstinacy. The arbitrary employment of masses resigned to their fate would become more difficult, and a prime factor in the typically Russian method of waging war would be lost. The force bringing about this change in the Russian soldier is Communism, or, more precisely, the spiritual awakening of the people, formerly so apathetic, by the rigid centralization of the entire State. The Russian is basically nonpolitical; at least that is true in the case of the rural population, which now as ever--but how much longer?--supplies the majority of soldiers. He is not an active Communist, not a political zealot. But he is--and here we already note a decisive change--a conscious Russian, who fights only in rare cases for any political ideals, but always for his fatherland.

11. In judging the basic qualities of the Russian it should be added that by nature he is brave, as he has well demonstrated in the course of his history. In 1807 it was the Russian soldier who for the first time, at Eylau, made a stand against Napoleon after the latter's victorious march through Europe; a stand which may be called almost epic.

12. In line with the awakening of the Russian soldier, another determining factor has been introduced into the Army by the political commissar--unqualified obedience. Carried out to the last word, it has made the raw mass of soldiers into a first-rate fighting machine. Systematic training, drill, disregard of one's own life, the natural inclination of the Russian soldier toward uncompromising subordination, and, not least of all, the unmistakable disciplinary powers available to the commissar, are the foundations of this ironclad obedience. In this connection, it must also be remembered that Russia is an autocratically ruled state with an absolute Fuehrerprinzip, demanding and, in case of necessity, compelling the complete subordination of the individual. That

blind obedience of the masses is the triumph of Communism, the mainspring of the Army, and the basic explanation of its successes. Armies with a less strict concept of obedience and discipline might very easily come out second best in a contest with these troops.

13. Another characteristic of the Russian soldier, in addition to the simplicity which corresponds to his limited household needs and his primitive mode of living, is his <u>close kinship with nature</u>. It can be stated without exaggeration that the Russian soldier is unaffected by season and terrain. This immunity gives him a decisive advantage over other soldiers, especially in Russian territory, where season, temperature, and terrain play a decisive role.

<u>Ex. 1</u>

14. In the attack the Russian fought unto death. Despite our most thorough defensive measures he would continue to go forward, completely disregarding losses. He was generally not subject to panic. For example, in the break-through of the fortifications before Bryansk in October 1941, enemy bunkers, which had long since been by-passed and which for days lay far behind our front, continued to be held when every hope of relief had vanished. Directly after the crossing of the Bug in July 1941, the fortifications which had been cleared of the enemy by the 167th Infantry Division were occupied a few days later by groups of stragglers, and subsequently had to be painstakingly retaken by a division which followed in the rear. An underground room in the heart of the citadel of Brest-Litovsk held out for many days against the 45th Infantry Division in spite of the employment of Stukas and the heaviest types of special guns.

15. The supply <u>problem</u> in the Russian Army is of secondary importance, because the Russian soldier requires only very few provisions for his own use. The field kitchen, a sacred institution to other troops, is for the Russians a pleasant surprise when it is available, but can be

dispensed with for days and weeks without undue hardship.

<u>Ex. 2</u>   16. During the winter campaign of 1941, a Russian regiment was surrounded in the woods along the Volkhov, and, because of the weakness of our forces, had to be starved out. After one week our reconnaissance patrols met with the same resistance as on the first day; after another week only a few prisoners were taken, the majority having fought their way through to their own troops in spite of close encirclement. According to the prisoners, the Russians subsisted during those weeks on a few pieces of frozen bread, leaves and pine needles--which they chewed--and some cigarettes. It had never occurred to anyone to throw in the sponge because of hunger, and the cold (-31° F) had not affected them. From a purely physical point of view only the Russian is capable of such a feat."

17. The kinship with nature, which the Russians have retained to a greater degree than the other peoples of Europe, is also responsible for the ability of the Russian soldier to adapt himself to terrain features, and actually to merge with them. He is a master of <u>camouflage</u>, <u>entrenchment</u>, and <u>defense construction</u>. With unbelievable speed he disappears into the earth, digging himself in with unfailing instinct so as to utilize the terrain to make his fortifications very difficult to discover. When the Russian has dug himself into his native soil and has molded himself into the landscape, he is a doubly dangerous opponent.

18. The utmost caution is required when <u>passing through unknown terrain</u>. Even long and searching observation often does not reveal the excellently camouflaged Russian. Frequently, German reconnaissance patrols passed through the immediate vicinity of Russian positions or individual riflemen without noticing them, and were then taken under fire from behind. Caution must be doubled in wooded terrain. In such areas the

Russians often disappear without a trace, and must be driven out individually, Indian fashion. Here, sniping from trees was particularly favored by the Russians as a method of fighting.

19. The forced industrialization of the country, carried out in a very short period of time, has made available to the Russian Army a large number of industrial workers with full command of technical skills. The Russian has mastered all new weapons and fighting equipment, all the requirements of machine warfare, with amazing rapidity. In this respect, too, the awakening of the Russian people has paid off. Soldiers trained in technical subjects, carefully distributed through the ranks, taught the necessary rudiments to their duller comrades, and to those who came from rural areas. This mastery was especially outstanding in the field of signal communications. The longer the war lasted, the better the Russians became at handling this type of equipment. Their own communications improved steadily, and with noteworthy skill the Russians soon made themselves familiar also with our signal communications. Monitoring and tuning in, jamming and deception, all these were arts which they understood very well. Whereas in World War I the telephone was still uncanny magic to the average Russian, he regarded the complicated radio set of World War II as an amusing toy. He maintained his iron discipline also in the field of signal communications, thereby propounding many a riddle for our own signal intelligence.

20. In contrast to the good side of the Russian soldier there were bad aspects of equal significance. It was one of the imponderables about each Russian unit whether good or bad would predominate.

The dawn has cast its first rays of light on the Russian masses, but it has not yet illuminated them. There still remains an appreciable residue of dullness, inflexibility, and apathy which it has not yet been possible to overcome, and which probably will not be overcome in the near future. Individual personalities rise above the masses.

21. The unpredictability of the mood of the Russian soldier, and his very pronounced herd instinct, make it possible for panics to arise suddenly in individual units. As often as one found it impossible to explain the fanatic resistance of individual units, as frequently did one encounter a mystery in their mass flights, or sudden, wholesale surrender. The reason may have been an imperceptible fluctuation in morale. Its effect could not be counteracted by any commissar.

22. His feelings drive the Russian into the group, which gives him strength and courage. The individual fighter created by modern warfare, of whom the German Army was composed, is rare among the Russians. In 80 out of 100 cases the Russian who has to stand on his own feet does not know what to do. This serious weakness of the Russian was compensated for by the large mass of men available. But what will happen once the Russian is compelled to fight simultaneously on several fronts, and those masses are not available everywhere?

23. A work concerning the craftiness of the Russian. He seldom employed ruses on a large scale. The usual tricks, such as feigning the existence of troops by increased fire and other means, were just as common with the Russians as with all armies of the world. They seldom carried out feint attacks. All the more, however, must one be on

guard against dishonesty and attempts at deception on the part of individual Russian soldiers and small units. One trick, a particular favorite, was feigning surrender, or coming over to the enemy with raised hands, white flags, and all the rest. Anyone approaching in good faith would very often be met with sudden surprise fire at close range. Feigning death is a trick often practiced by the Russian soldier, who can lie motionless for hours on end. An unguarded approach often costs one's life.

Chapter Two

THE RUSSIAN COMMAND ECHELONS

24. The <u>higher echelons of command</u> proved capable from the very beginning of the war and learned a great deal more during its course. They were flexible, full of initiative, and energetic. However, they were unable to inspire the great mass of Russian soldiers.

25. Most of the commanders had been advanced in peacetime to positions of authority at a very early age, although there were some older men among them. All social levels were represented, from the common laborer to the university professor of Mongolian languages and cultures. Of course, merit in the Revolution played a part, yet one had the impression that the choice was well made with respect to character, military understanding, and intelligence. Purely party generals apparently had been given positions carrying little more than prestige. The <u>extraordinary industry</u> with which these commanders went about their duties was characteristic. Every day, and far into the night, they sat together to discuss and to record in writing what they had seen and heard during the day.

26. During the various <u>political purges</u> an appreciable portion of this command strata disappeared. But it was a mistake to assume that a deterioration of the higher command had resulted. Military education in Russia, on the basis of precepts which were largely taken over from us, had made such great progress that even the higher commanders

available at the beginning of the war were of a stature commensurate with their duties. It must in this connection be noted that a nation as young, energetic, and populous as Russia, was able to draw on an inexhaustible source of strength. In addition, this group of officers was held in high regard by the populace, was extolled in propaganda, and was very comfortably situated economically. Many things testified to the position which the higher military leaders of the Soviet Union enjoyed in the State and among the people: pictures in prewar Russian illustrated newspapers; the display in Soviet Army office buildings of artistically valuable portraits of senior officers, and of paintings showing episodes in their military careers; and the exhibition on stairways and in government buildings of banners emblazoned with the pronouncements of high-ranking military officers. Our propaganda misunderstood and misrepresented much.

27. Many developments in the sphere of strategy, which now and then gave rise to doubts about the ability of these leaders, require an examination of their background before they can be properly judged. The alleged failure during the Finnish winter campaign of 1939-40 played a large part, but nevertheless, as much as the Finns disliked hearing it, the conjecture cannot be dismissed that there was a great deal of bluffing involved. The timing of the operation was correct and had to produce results as soon as the will of the immeasurably superior attacker desired them. That fact does not belittle the heroic display of courage by the Finnish people in the struggle.

28. Neither is the success of our surprise attack at the

MS # T-22   -17-

opening of the campaign against Russia in 1941 any proof to the contrary. A later generation will have to examine, and will perhaps be able to decide, to what extent the Soviets wanted to be surprised. Along the Central Front, and also in the North, one had the impression that the actual war did not begin until the Dnepr and the Luga had been reached. Timoshenko's strategic war game, as well as the course of events at the beginning of the Eastern Campaign, substantiate this assumption.

Ex. 3

App. 1

29. In mid-July 1941, the LIII Infantry Corps joined in the defensive battle in the Dnepr--Beresina triangle against Timoshenko's thrust into the flank and rear of Panzer Group 2, which was advancing on Smolensk. Soon thereafter, Corps found out that in <u>February 1941</u>, in a Komsomol home on the Bobruisk--Rogachev road, Timoshenko and higher commanders had held a <u>conference which lasted several days</u>. Upon exhaustive search, a map was found in that home, marked as follows: German armored units were assumed to be north of Rogachev, east of the Dnepr. A pincers operation was being launched against them from the regions of Zhlobin--Rogachev and Mogilev, with Bobruisk as the objective. A very strong group of forces was to advance to the northwest via Zhlobin--Rogachev, another of like strength to the southwest via Mogilev, and cut off the German armor. The two groups were to meet at Bobruisk. The intermediate daily objectives of the two groups were indicated by semicircles. A cavalry unit with three elements, committed on the west bank of the Beresina and striking northward from the Parichi area, was to cut the Slutsk--Bobruisk road and the Minsk--Bobruisk railroad, and complete the encirclement.

Since the armored units had already defeated the northern enemy group near Orsha, there remained only the southern arm of the pincers. With a total of twenty divisions, Timoshenko carried through this part of the operation that apparently had been planned in February. He thus came in contact with LIII Infantry Corps, which had in the meantime arrived in the Dnepr--

Beresina triangle by way of Bobruisk. There developed a bitter 3-week defense action between the Corps--comprising three divisions--and those Russian forces which had advanced across the Dnepr near Zhlobin and Rogachev. During the course of this battle, the cavalry corps indicated on the map also appeared, and for a while actually reached its objectives. The LIII Infantry Corps was cut off from the rear for about a week.

30. Customs and frontier guards on the Bug; very weak enemy forces after a few days; finally the big battle in the Dnepr--Beresina triangle: thus began the Eastern Campaign. Prisoner statements furnished a very clear picture of the preliminaries, concentrations, and groupings for the battle on the Russian side. Again and again they gave the impression that large-scale enemy movements did not get under way until after the opening of the campaign, and that they took place beyond the Dnepr. From the viewpoint of Russian grand strategy it was undoubtedly an expedient solution. (Our own intelligence service, to be sure, identified continuous troop movements to the Russo-German frontier as early as spring of 1940, supposedly involving 130 divisions even at that time.)

31. The events which led up to the battle of Uman on the Southern Front offer no damaging proof against the Russian higher command, but show only the danger and the detrimental effect of injecting politics into current military operations.

32. Thus the Russian higher command was, by and large, fully competent. Whether Timoshenko's tenacity in carrying out his plan--as mentioned in Example 3 above, even though the northern part

of the pincers operation was knocked out, should be regarded as inflexibility, or whether Timoshenko considered that there were possibilities for a great success just the same, is not up for discussion. During the subsequent course of the war, however, a flexibility in strategy was apparent in the Russian higher command that, in tactics, long remained unknown in the performace of the intermediate and lower command echelons. An awareness of responsibility accompanied the willingness to accept responsibility.

Ex. 4

33. After the break-through of LIII Infantry Corps from the southwest to Bryansk at the beginning of October 1941, the opposing Fiftieth Russian Army, commanded by General Petrov, withdrew, badly shaken, to the wooded terrain northeast of Bryansk. The Bryansk pocket was the result. During the withdrawal the commander of the Fiftieth Army had been given command of Army Group Bryansk, under which, in addition to the Fiftieth Army, were placed the Thirtieth and Thirty-third Armies. The diary of Major Shabalin, a State Security (GPU) officer attached to Fiftieth Army Headquarters who was killed in the Bryansk pocket, contained approximately the following on the subject:

I (Shabalin) congratulated General Petrov at breakfast upon his appointment as commander of Army Group Bryansk. General Petrov answered only: "So now they are going to shoot me too." I replied: "How can you talk of shooting? Your appointment as commander of the Group is an indication of confidence in your ability to get things organized again." General Petrov: "How can I get the situation back under control when I don't know where the Thirtieth and Thirty-third Armies are and what condition they are in?"

A few days later General Petrov was killed in the Bryansk pocket at the side of Major Shabalin, State Security officer.

34. If, as seen in the previous example, the newly appointed commander of Army Group Bryansk, instead of rejoicing, sadly stated that he had no idea where the armies newly entrusted to him were, or what condition they were in, and that he, therefore, from a practical standpoint was unable to fulfill what was expected of him, then such a reaction represents a conscious sense of responsibility and a genuine soldierly demeanor. Marshal Kulik, with a serious leg injury, supported himself on a cane and led the 10,000 men which he had reassembled after the Minsk pocket through the swamps near Bobruisk, and gave the German troops a lot of trouble. The higher Red Army commanders have never spared themselves.

35. The way operations were launched and carried out revealed the German influence on the Soviet higher command. Operations against flank and rear, large-scale envelopments, and encirclements all played a part. Other maneuvers employed were mobile defense and, finally, break-through and break-out.

36. Timoshenko's plan for a double envelopment and isolation of our large armored units which had advanced across the Dnepr undoubtedly was on the grand scale. The operation also was carried out energetically and efficiently. The strategic concentration, assembly, and commitment of units participating in the attack were irreproachable according to German concepts.

37. The great thrust via Yefremov at the beginning of November 1941, in which the Russians aimed at the rear of our armored units standing in front of Tula, and which later led to the battle of annihila-

tion southeast of Plavskoye, was likewise well planned. From a strategic and tactical point of view it had a chance of success. The weakest point of our armored thrust had been recognized and correctly exploited.

38. Altogether it cannot be denied that the Russian higher command had an eye for strategically and tactically weak points of the enemy. The battle of Moscow in 1941-42 and its consequences are just as good an example of this as, on a smaller scale, the operation on the Kandalaksha front in northern Finland against XXXVI Mountain Corps late in the winter of 1944. (Ed: See App. 3.) The Red Army higher command can, of course, claim more and even greater successes, such as the various major offensives from 1943 to 1945.

39. To be sure, the Soviet command had an easier time of it than we did, because the resources of their own country and a large number of troop units were available to them. Equipment, training, and physical and spiritual character of their armed forces all corresponded to the conditions in the East. For this reason, a great number of endless difficulties, which caused us all sorts of trouble, simply did not exist for the Russian higher command. In addition, a low valuation of human life gave the higher command a greater freedom from inhibitions. Whether, for example, several divisions were lost in an encirclement, or whether a reindeer division on the Murmansk front perished in a snowstorm, was of no particular importance. Not until later did the long duration of the war and the extensive losses force them to greater economy of manpower.

40. The lower command echelons of the Russian Army, and for the most part also the intermediate echelons*, remained for a long

---

*Ed: According to the German field service regulations (Heeresdienstvorschriften 300/1, Truppenfuehrung, 1943): "Command echelons are divided into higher and lower command. Higher command includes units down through infantry and cavalry divisions; lower command includes all smaller units."

Generalmajor Hellmuth Reinhardt (CofS, General Army Office, German Army High Command, Mar 41-Oct 43) writes in MS # P-015 that the term "intermediate echelons" (mittlere Fuehrung) was a German military colloquialism for command at division level and, sometimes, at corps level; in rare cases, the term also included regimental level.

---

period inflexible and indecisive, avoiding all personal responsibility. The rigid pattern of training, and an overly strict discipline, so narrowly confined the lower command within the framework of existing regulations that the result was lethargy. Spirited application to a task, born of the decision of an individual, was a rarity. Russian elements that had broken through our lines could remain for days behind our front without recognizing their favorable position and taking advantage of it. Their presence was an inconvenience, but one could be practically certain that they would do no harm. The Russian small unit commander's fear of doing something wrong and being called to account for it was greater than the urge to take advantage of a situation.

41. The commanders of Russian combined-arms units were actually well trained along tactical lines, but to some extent they had not grasped the essence of tactical doctrines, and therefore often acted according to set patterns, not according to circumstances. Also, there was the pronounced spirit of blind obedience, which had perhaps carried over

from civilian life into the military field. Thus, for example, toward the end of September 1941, in the area southwest of Bryansk, the same sector was attacked by various Russian battalions every day for seven days running without any apparent reason and without success, but with severe losses. Finally, a captured battalion commander supplied the explanation. In looking through some old files, their new regimental commander had found a top-level order to the effect that continuous attacks were to be made along the entire front in order to ease the pressure on Leningrad. Since he had received a negative answer to his inquiry as to whether these attacks had already been made, he had ordered this sector attacked every day. In the meantime, however, two months had passed, and the pressure on Leningrad had long since been relieved.

42. This lethargy and reluctance to assume responsibility was a serious drawback to the Red Army, completely neutralizing a great many good points of the Russian soldier. Later on, the Soviet commanders learned a great deal along this line and became more flexible. The tactical employment of the 6th Rifle Division in the battle of annihilation southeast of Plavskoye may be termed perfect: advance, withdrawal in trucks in dangerous situations, another forward thrust, and then attack.

43. According to statements of prisoners and monitored telephone conversations, the Russian command faced the same problems we and probably other armies faced so far as care of the troops and internal administration were concerned. There was great interest in hygienic measures. But also other matters, such as decorations, promotions, results

of the war loan, and similar matters, kept the lower commanders very busy.

Chapter Three

THE COMMISSAR

44. The commissar was probably the most controversial element in the Russian Army. Even in the Soviet Union itself opinions varied concerning his usefulness, his position, and his duties. The following picture has been pieced together from numerous captured files of the commissars, from the diary of Major Shabalin of the State Security Service, from the observed effect of their work, and from statements of prisoners. * * *

45. The influence of the Party and of its representatives in the Army--the commissars or Politruks--was tremendous. They were the driving force of the Army. The commissars ruled with cunning, cold-bloodedness, and force. By means of a close-meshed network of especially chosen personalities, they held the entire army machine under their control and in a tight grip. The commissars were to a preponderant degree real political fanatics. They came mostly from the working class, were almost without exception city people, brave, intelligent, and unscrupulous. But they also took care of the troops. Even though, during the course of the war, their intervention in the military conduct of the war was reduced, thanks to Stalin's military instinct, their influence was not lessened thereby.

46. However, it is not true that the Russian soldier fought so well only because of fear of the commissars, under the pressure of the

machine guns set up behind him and manned by Politruks. A soldier who is motivated solely by fear can never have the qualities that the Russian soldier of this war displayed. The motive of fear may often have been the final resort in difficult situations, but basically the Russian has no less national--as distinguished from political--ethos than the soldier of the Western armies, and with it the same source of strength. Unceasing propaganda has burned nationalism into his soul. And however impervious he may be to foreign propaganda, he nevertheless has been unable to escape the engulfing waves of his own.

47. Among the troops themselves the relationship of the soldier to the commissar apparently was still endurable, in spite of his uncompromising strictness and severity. The higher headquarters, on the other hand, appear to have regarded him with mistrust. Testimony to that conclusion is found not only in the episode mentioned in Example 5 below, between a young officer of a division headquarters and the division commissar, but also in many remarks of the commander of the Fiftieth Army, General Petrov, to Shabalin, which the latter recorded verbatim in his diary. Thus, General Petrov once ironically asked Shabalin, who was sitting next to him in the tank: "Well, how many have you shot today?" Shabalin added the note: "Such sarcasm." The commissar was thus often considered an alien element by headquarters.

Ex. 5   48. On the battlefield of Bryansk the records of a division commissar were captured, among them the carbon copies of reports to a higher political office in Moscow.

MS # T-22

In one of these carbon copies was the following account. The prohibition of vodka in the Russian Army, which had been in effect until then, was rescinded in August 1941. The division commissar recommended the immediate restoration of the prohibition and based his recommendation on the following occurrence at his division headquarters: The first liquor to arrive was not distributed to the troops by division headquarters, but used by the headquarters staff itself. The result was general drunkenness among the staff members one evening. The officers allegedly went out into the village street and killed geese with their pistols. When there were no more geese, a officer of division headquarters pounded him—the commissar—on the shoulder and said, "Well, all the geese have been shot dead. Now it's your turn, Politruk." This was proof that a complete prohibition of liquor would have to be re-established in the army as quickly as possible.

* * *

Ex. 6

49. In the fighting east of Roslavl in August 1941, a Russian tank company that had been sent into action suddenly stopped dead on the battlefield. From statements of prisoners it was learned that the leader of the tank company had received an order before going into action to refuel at a fuel depot somewhat to the rear of his bivouac area. He did not, however, want to bother going back and thought that it would be possible to refuel farther forward at the divisional command post nearer the front. But there was no opportunity to refuel at that point. The tank company just reached the battlefield and then ground to a halt. Thereupon the company commissar drew his pistol and shot the first lieutenant on the spot.

* * *

50. The attitude of the common man toward the commissar was conditioned not only by fear of his power, but also by his personal exemplification of the soldier and fighter. His concern for the welfare of the troops also determined to a large extent his relationship with the men. In all the captured reports dealing with the activity of the commissars there was considerable mention made of the condition of the troops.

Shabalin, for instance, reported to higher authority the insufferable conditions on the Moscow--Orel--Bryansk railroad. Thus, for example, he immediately sent a division commissar, whom, while reconnoitering for new division headquarters, he discovered in the rear, back to the front with the observation: "You belong with your troops; go and take care of them." Innumerable recommendations for the improvement of conditions in the army hospitals were found among captured papers.

* * *

51. The example set by the commissars is largely responsible for the tenacious resistance of the Russian soldier, even in hopeless situations. It would be wrong to believe that the German Commissar Order (Ed: directing that, upon capture, commissars be turned over to the SS Security Service (Sicherheitsdienst) for "special treatment", i.e., execution) was solely responsible for inciting the commissars to bitter last-ditch resistance; the impetus much rather was fanaticism together with soldierly qualities, and probably also the feeling of responsibility for the victory of the Soviet Union. The previously mentioned occupation of the bunkers on the Bug and the continued resistance in the citadel of Brest-Litovsk can be traced to the influence of the commissars.

* * *

52. In innumerable other cases, too, dogged perseverance even under hopeless conditions was to be credited to the soldierly conduct of the commissars. For instance, in September 1941, long after the castle of Posyolok Taytsy (south of Leningrad) had been taken, and strong troop units drawn up in the castle park, tanks passing near the park wall with open hatches drew single rounds of rifle fire from close

range. The shots were aimed at the unprotected tank commanders who were looking out of the turrets. Not until three of them had been killed by bullets through the head did the passing tank unit realize that the deadly shots were coming from a narrow trench close under the park wall ten meters away. The tanks now returned the fire, whereupon all thirteen occupants of the trench met death. They were the officers of the regimental headquarters grouped about their commissar, who fell with his rifle cocked and aimed.

53. After panzer divisions broke out of the Luga bridgeheads in August 1941, the commander of a task force (Kampfgruppe) inspected several Russian tanks which had been knocked out two hours earlier near a church. A large number of men were looking on. Suddenly, the turret of one of the knocked-out tanks began to revolve and fire. The tank had to be blown up. It turned out that among the crew, which had been assumed dead, there was a commissar who had merely been unconscious. When he revived and saw the many German soldiers around him, he opened fire.

54. When in April 1942 a strong enemy position was taken along the Osuga (southwest of Rzhev), the attackers continued to receive rifle fire from one lone barricaded bunker. All demands for surrender were in vain. When an attempt was made to shoot through the embrasure with a rifle, the enemy grabbed it and fired the last three shots. Two of them wounded German soldiers, and the commissar, who was defending the bunker alone in the midst of his dead comrades, shot himself with the third.

55. One might well be of the opinion that much of the fighting spirit and concern for the welfare of the troops which the commissars displayed should have been the responsibility of the commanding officers and not of the commissars. However, as it appeared from captured records and from battle experiences, it was always a question of situations in which something had to be done. The commanding officers generally did nothing much, but the commissars acted. The passive character of the Russians was responsible for the fact that it was not the commander but the commissar who discovered the road to action. Therefore, the commissar was really a necessary part in the structure of the Red Army. He was a sort of <u>frontline conscience.</u>

56. It is difficult for the Russians themselves to properly judge this matter, and much more so for anyone more distantly removed. Rejecting from the very outset an institution which also had its good points under prevailing conditions would be a mistake.

57. The commissars found special support among the women who served within the framework of the Soviet Army. The following example illustrates their political and military conduct.

* * *

Ex. 7   58. Russian women served in all-female units with the so-called partisan bands, or individually as gunners in the artillery, as spies dropped by parachute, as medical corps aides with the fighting troops, or in the rear in the auxiliary services. They were political fanatics, filled with hate for every opponent, cruel, and incorruptible. The women were enthusiastic Communists, and dangerous.

59. It was also not unusual for women to fight in the front lines. Thus, uniformed women took part in the final break-out struggle at Sevastopol in 1942; medical corps women in 1941 defended the last positions in front of Leningrad with pistols and hand grenades, until they fell in the battle. (See Example 22.) In the fighting along the middle Donets in February 1943, a Russian tank was apparently rendered immobile by a direct hit. When our own tanks approached, it suddenly reopened fire and attempted to break out. A second direct hit again brought it to a standstill, but in spite of its hopeless position it defended itself while a tank-killer team advanced upon it, until it finally burst into flame from a demolition charge. Only then did the turret hatch open. A woman in tanker uniform climbed out. She was the wife and co-fighter of a tank company commander, who, killed by the first hit, lay beside her in the turret.

60. So far as the soldiers were concerned, women in uniform were superiors or comrades to whom respect was paid.

* * *

61. The four elements which determine the nature of Russian warfare—the higher command, the troops, the commissar, and the Russian territory—fitted together in such a way that their combination was responsible for good performance and great successes. The weakest elements were the intermediate and lower command echelons. Their shortcomings, however, were made up for in part by appropriate action on the part of the higher command, and by the good will, the discipline, the undemanding nature, and the self-sacrificing devotion to duty of the men under the influence of energetic commissars, who were filled with a belief in the essential necessity of victory. The Russian soldier thereby became an instrument which provided his leaders with the sort of fighter they needed for their operations.

Chapter Four
THE COMBAT ARMS

I. <u>Infantry</u>

62. The characterization of the Russian soldier presented up to this point applies primarily to the infantry. This branch of service supplied the bulk of fighting men in active combat, and most clearly exemplified the peculiar characteristics of the Russian.

63. The Red Army infantry was for a long period of time the mainstay of the Russian fighting machine, and in the Arctic it continued as such until the end of the war. As is apparent from the previously described characteristics of the Russian soldier, the Soviet infantry was willing, undemanding, suitable trained and equipped, and, above all, brave and endowed with a self-sacrificing devotion to duty. The Bolshevist philosophy appeared to have become firmly rooted among the great mass of younger people, and to have made them loyal soldiers, differing in their perseverance and performance from those of World War I. The Russian infantryman, subject to rapidly changing moods, was jovial one moment, cruel the next. However, the fighters in the Arctic, natives of the northern parts of Russia, were fair-playing opponents throughout.

64. The Russian infantryman was a member of the herd, preferring to fight in concert with others rather than to be left to his own devices. In the attack, this characteristic was evidenced in the

massed lines, sometimes almost packs; in the defense we witnessed it in the stubbornly resisting bunker complements. Here, there was no individual action for one's personal advantage. The soldiers aided each other and, as was gathered from monitored telephone conversations, even displayed an interest in their comrades' family affairs.

* * *

65. It has already been pointed out that the Russian soldier was as good as immune to seasonal and terrain difficulties. Further, he was almost complete master of the terrain. There appeared to be no terrain obstacles for the infantryman. He was as much at home in dense forest as in swamp or trackless steppe. Difficult terrain features stopped him for only a limited time. Even the broad Russian streams were crossed quickly with the aid of the most primitive expedients. It could never be assumed that the Russian would be held back by terrain normally considered impassable. It was in just such places that his appearance, and frequently his attack, had to be expected. The infantryman could, if he chose, completely overcome terrain obstacles in a very short time. Kilometers of corduroy road were laid through marshy terrain in a few days; paths were tramped through forests covered with deep snow. Ten men abreast, with arms interlocked, and in ranks 100 deep, prepared these lanes in 15-minute reliefs of 1,000 men each. Teams of innumerable infantrymen moved guns and heavy weapons wherever they were needed. During the winter, snow caves which could be heated were constructed to furnish night shelter for men and horses. The Russian materiel was useful in this respect: motorization reduced to an absolute minimum; the lightest

vehicles; tough horses that required little care; suitable uniforms; and, finally, again the human mass which moved all loads and performed all required tasks like a machine.

66. A singular kinship to nature made the Russian infantryman an ideal fighter in forests, barren country, and swamps. In the Arctic, small units of several men stayed for weeks in the desolate area in our rear. Female radio operators attached to those units were treated with particular respect.

67. Wounds were endured patiently and without complaint. Frostbite was a punishable offense because it was avoidable. Recovery, even from serious injuries, was rapid. Many an injury that would have been fatal to a Central European was endured and overcome.

68. The best weapon of the Russian infantryman was the machine pistol. It was an easily handled weapon equal to Russian winter conditions, and one which we also regarded highly. This weapon was slung around the neck and carried in front of the chest ready for immediate action. The mortar also proved highly valuable: the ideal weapon for terrain conditions where artillery support was impossible. At the beginning of the Eastern Campaign, Russian infantry far surpassed us in mortar equipment and in its use. The same was true for the Russian antitank gun, which at the beginning of the campaign considerably surpassed the antitank gun of our infantry divisions in efficiency, and therefore was readily put to use by us whenever we captured it.

✗ ✗ ✗

69. The antitank gun was an auxiliary weapon from which the Russian soldier never separated. Wherever the Russian infantryman

was, antitank defense could be expected. At times it appeared that each Russian infantryman had an antitank gun or antitank rifle, just as infantrymen of other armies had ordinary rifles. The Russian moved his antitank defense everywhere with great skill. It was to be found even where no enemy tank attacks might be expected. Emplacements were set up within a few minutes. If the small gun--always excellently camouflaged--was not needed for antitank defense, its flat trajectory and great accuracy were put to good use in infantry combat. For this reason, the following rule is again expressed: Engage Russian infantry immediately following their appearance, for shortly thereafter not only the soldier but also his antitank defense will have disappeared into the ground, and every countermeasure will be twice as costly.

70. The Russian infantryman had a noteworthy negative characteristic: He was not inquisitive. His <u>reconnaissance</u> often was extremely poor. Combat patrols were for him the means of gathering information about the enemy whenever he thought it necessary. Although the Russian proved himself an excellent scout, he made too little use of his abilities in this field. The higher Russian command was always well informed on the enemy situation by means of radio monitoring, interrogation of prisoners, captured documents, and other means. But the intermediate and lower commanders apparently were only slightly interested in their opponents. Here again the cause lay in the lack of self-reliance and in the individual Russian infantryman's inability to assemble into a useful report the observations made while on patrol.

71. <u>Clothing</u> and <u>equipment</u> of the Russian infantry suited summer as well as winter requirements of the East. We were amazed at how excellently the Siberian infantry was clothed in the winter of 1941-42. As might be expected, the fighters in the Arctic were likewise suitably clothed. The Russian infantryman was inferior to us and to the Finns only in his skiing. Of course, attempts were made to correct this deficiency through intensified training, but all efforts were doomed to failure since there was never more than one pair of skis available for several men.

72. Equipment that we always carried was discarded by the Russian infantryman, so long as it did not seem absolutely essential. Most Russian gas masks were stored in division depots. Steel helmets were seldom seen in the wilderness of the Far North.

II. <u>Artillery</u>

73. The efficiency of the Russian artillery varied greatly during the various stages of the war. In the beginning it was unable to achieve an effective concentration of fire, and, furthermore, was unenthusiastic about firing on targets in the depth of the battle position even when there was excellent observation. The Rogachev water tower, for example, and the railroad control towers as well as the high railroad embankment at Zhlobin, all of which were in Russian hands during the battle in the Dnepr--Beresina triangle, commanded a view over the entire area for many kilometers; nevertheless, they were not used for directing fire on very important

targets behind our lines. On the Kandalaksha front, continuous supply transport operations at the Karhu railroad station took place within sight of Russian observation posts. These operations were never taken under fire by enemy artillery. On the other hand, the Russian artillery liked to distribute its fire over the front lines, and occasionally shelled a road intersection located not too far from the front.

74. During the course of the war the artillery, too, developed to a high degree the use of <u>mass</u> as a particularly characteristic procedure. Infantry attacks without artillery preparation were rare. Short preparatory concentrations lasting only a few minutes, frequently employed on the German side in order to preserve the element of surprise, seemed insufficient to the Russians. Thus, counting on the destructive effect of their massed fire, they consciously accepted the fact that we would recognize their intentions of attacking. Russian artillery fire often had no primary target, but covered the entire area with the same intensity. The Russian artillery was very vulnerable to counterbattery fire. It ceased firing, or changed position, after only a few rounds from our guns. The rigidity of the fire plan, and a certain immobility of the Soviet artillery--at least during the first years of the war--was pronounced. Only in rare cases was the artillery successful in promptly following the infantry. Most of the time the artillery was unable to follow up; it remained stuck in the old positions, leaving the infantry without fire support. This practice frequently took the momentum out of the Russian attacks.

      ※   ※   ※

75. <u>Attack tactics</u> of the Russian artillery improved con-

stantly during the war. Eventually, however, their tactics resolved into an ever-repeated, set scheme. Heavy preparatory fire, laid down broad and deep and lasting from one to two hours, was the initial phase; it rapidly mounted to murderous intensity. Once an attack was about to get under way, the Russians suddenly lifted their fire from very narrow lanes (about 80 to 100 meters wide), along which the infantry was to advance. At all other points the fire continued with undiminished fury. Only the most careful observation allowed recognition of those lanes. In most instances one had the impression that artillery preparation was still continuing in full force, though in reality the infantry attack had already begun. Here again, we found the same concept: human lives mean nothing at all. If our defensive fire forced the Russian infantry out of their narrow lanes, or if their own artillery was unable to maintain the lanes accurately--Nichevo!--those were operating expenses.

76. It must be admitted that, despite many shortcomings, the Russian artillery was a very good and extremely dangerous arm. Its fire was effective, rapid, and accurate, and it was always a mistake to regard it without due respect. Particularly during the Russian large-scale attacks in the summer of 1944 did it become apparent that the enemy had learned well how to mass and employ large artillery units. Establishment of a definite point of main effort and the use of superior masses of artillery crushed the thin lines of German opposition at many places at the Eastern Front before the actual attack had begun. This successful procedure of establishing definite points of main effort will be used by the Russians also in the future whenever they have the masses

MS # T-22   -39-

of artillery and ammunition required. For a countermeasure which we employed with success see MSS # T-10 and T-21.

III. Armored Force

77. The heart of the Russian armored force was the well-known T 34 tank--an outstanding engineering feat--which might be termed an all-purpose tank. Because of its wide tracks, its powerful engine, and its low silhouette, the performance of the T 34 in Russian terrain was frequently superior to that of the German tanks, particularly with respect to cross-country mobility. To the surprise of all the experts, the T 34 easily negotiated terrain theoretically secure against mechanized attack. The caliber of its guns was too small, however, and forced the Russians to produce several new types of tanks (KV I, Stalin), which, like the German models, became successively heavier. Despite all improvements, however, the new tanks remained on the whole inferior to the T 34. The Russians, too, recognized this fact, and continued to mass produce the T 34 until the end of the war.

78. Not until late did the Russians decide on launching concerted attacks by large tank forces. During the first years of the war, Russian tanks generally were used for local infantry support. Soviet tank attacks as such took place only after a sufficient number of the vehicles had become available. Here, too, the Russians adhered to their usual habit of employing great masses of men and machines.

79. Tank attacks generally were not conducted at a fast enough pace. Frequently they were not well enough adapted to the nature

of the terrain. Those facts we noted time and again, up to the end of the war.

80. The **training** of the individual tank drivers was inadequate; the training period apparently was too short, and losses of experienced drivers were too high. The Russian avoided driving his tank through hollows or along reverse slopes, preferring to choose a route along the crests that would present fewer driving difficulties. This practice remained unchanged even in the face of unusually high tank losses. Thus the defense was in most cases able to bring the Russian tanks under fire at long range, and to inflict losses on them even before the battle had begun. Slow and uncertain driving, and numerous firing halts, made the Russian tanks good targets. Premature firing on the Russian tanks, though wrong in principle, was always the correct solution in those instances. If the defense was ready and adequate, the swarms of Russian tanks began to thin out very quickly in most cases. True, this fault in Russian tank tactics can be corrected by peacetime training, but it can hardly be totally eliminated.

81. On the whole, the Russian armored force does not merit commendation equal to that due the Russian artillery. Limited flexibility, and the inability of the subordinate commanders to exploit favorable situations rapidly and adroitly, were evident also here, and frequently prevented the Russians from achieving successes almost within their grasp. Toward the end of the war, however, the inadequate facilities of the poor contender no longer were able to stand up against the masses of equipment of the rich opponent, and the latter was able to roll

along as he wished. Thus, for example, on 1 March 1945 a mere 70 German tanks faced 1,600 Russian tanks in the battle of Pomerania.

* * *

IV. <u>Horse Cavalry</u>

82. In the Russian theater of operations the cavalry, despite many changes in tactics and equipment, achieved a significance reminiscent of old times. In our army, all cavalry except one lone division had been replaced by panzer units. That was a mistake so far as the Eastern Campaign was concerned. The Russian successfully followed another course. The LIII Infantry Corps quite often encountered Russian cavalry divisions, and once a cavalry corps comprising three cavalry elements--always in situations in which cavalry was a suitable arm for the enemy's purpose.

83. In the battle in the Dnepr--Beresina triangle, a cavalry corps comprising three elements appeared west of the Beresina near Bobruisk, out of the Pripyat Marshes, in the rear of the German corps which was engaged in hard fighting. This cavalry force cut the Slutsk--Bobruisk highway and the Minsk--Bobruisk railroad, and thereby isolated the corps for a week from its supply and contact with the rear. Bobruisk itself, together with the bridges there, was seriously threatened. Only by prompt emergency measures were we able to ease the pressure. During that period the corps ammunition supply dropped to twenty rounds per light field howitzer (<u>Ed</u>: 105 mm.), and that at a time when Timoshenko's major offensive had reached its peak. Forces other than cavalry would have been unable to conduct such a raid.

84. In the advance out of the Bryansk pocket northward

past Plavskoye to the upper Don in October–November 1941, the 112th Infantry Division of LIII Infantry Corps was met by a Russian cavalry divison just as it reached the Orel--Tula road. There ensued some very unpleasant delays. The cavalry division accomplished its mission by occupying every town along the route of advance, withdrawing from each one as soon as the Division advanced to attack. Thus the 112th Division was kept occupied by constant small-scale warfare.

85. During the battle of annihilation southeast of Plavskoye, cavalry divisions appeared on both wings of the Russian attack front. The cavalry division just mentioned was on the northern wing. The Russian higher command had diverted it to the battlefield as soon as the 112th Infantry Division turned in that direction. But the cavalry division, with its greater speed, reached the Plavskoye area ahead of the 112th Division and blocked its advance until a Russian rifle division arrived at the front. The cavalry division mentioned earlier was on the southern wing. That division was to reach the Orel--Tula express motor highway in a forced march so as to cut it near Chern--under prevailing circumstances a handsome and practicable task for a cavalry division.

86. The Corps' further advance to the upper Don was constantly accompanied and watched by a cavalry division ten to twenty kilometers off its right flank. The cavalry division would have been able to intervene at once, in any manner whatsoever, if the Russian higher command had had any occasion for ordering it to do so.

87. The above examples are drawn from situations in which the missions in question could have been executed only by cavalry.

Our armored vehicles were laid up in October during the muddy period. Only cavalry could operate through the Pripyat Marshes.

88. Under Eastern conditions, as characterized in Central Russia by great forest and swamp areas, muddy periods, and deep snow, cavalry is an arm without peer. Where the motor failed, the horse's legs continued to move. The conduct of the cavalry forces was, however, not always suited to the situation and sometimes was even awkward. Leadership and training in the Russian cavalry were not up to the World War I standard.

Chapter Five
RUSSIAN COMBAT METHODS

89. Just as the Russian soldier had his own peculiarities in his internal make-up, so did he have them in his combat methods. The most common Russian form of combat was the use of mass. Human mass and mass of materiel were generally used unintelligently and without variation, but they were always effective. Both had to be available before they could be used lavishly; they were therefore dependent upon limitless Russian supplies. The Russian disdain for life--always present, but now infinitely heightened by Communism--favored this practice. One must never believe that a Russian attack which has been twice repulsed with unheard-of losses will not be repeated a third and a fourth time at the same place and in the same fashion. Unimpressed by previous failures and losses, new waves always came on. An unusual inflexibility of mind and unimaginative obstinacy lay in this use of masses, and was dearly paid for. It will never be possible to estimate Russian war casualties with any degree of accuracy; there will always be a potential error of many hundred thousands. This inflexible method of warfare, with the objective of accomplishing everything through the use of human masses, is the most inhuman and costly possible.

90. Characteristic of the disdain for human life was the complete elimination of funeral rites. There was no such thing as a funeral ceremony for the ordinary citizen in Communist Russia. It ran

counter to her antireligious philosophy and the mass sacrifice of human beings. The cemeteries dating from the era of Christian Russia had for the most part disappeared, or were completely neglected. Weather-worn fragments of stone, or little irregularities in the ground under which were buried the rotted stumps of sawed-off wooden crosses, were the last witnesses in the East of a bygone belief in the life hereafter. On the other hand, hundreds of birch crosses bearing the names of German dead frequently lined the perimeters of towns, forests, and roads which earlier had been battlegrounds. Former town cemeteries, and grounds around hospitals and churches, were often dotted with thousands of such crosses, and were well tended. Here and there, on a high mound of earth, there rose a heavy wooden cross erected by German soldiers, bearing the inscription, "Here lie 275 Russian soldiers." Those were the only tokens that honored the heroism of Russian common soldiers. Of course, there were also the burial mounds in which a thick peg, painted red, had been driven into the ground at the head end, inscribed with the heroic deeds of some commissar killed in action. The bulk of the dead millions were unceremoniously plowed under. Thus, all outward indications of the number of dead were obliterated.

91. A typical example occurred before Leningrad in September 1941. Accustomed to this type of burial, prisoners of war and civilians--old men, women, and children--charged with the interment of three hundred Russian dead, loaded the bodies on Panje wagons (peasant carts), and tossed them into three trench graves. When they noticed that there was no room left for the last thirty or forty bodies, they tramped on the

corpses with their boots until there was enough room. They finished this work with childish glee on their faces, happy that they had saved themselves the trouble of digging another hole.

92. Not until 1944 did the Russians start using their men a bit more sparingly. Only after there were no new millions available to the Russians could one detect in their orders the first reference to consideration in the use of men, and admonitions to avoid losses. Nevertheless, a thinning of attack waves was virtually unknown to the Russians until almost the last days of the war. The herd instinct and lack of self-reliance on the part of the subordinate commanders time and again misled them into the concentrated employment of troops. It was not particularly difficult to crush the attack of the human mass so long as the opposition possessed a mass of materiel in trained hands.

93. In the winter of 1941, the Russians cleared a German mine field south of Leningrad by chasing over it tightly closed columns of unarmed Russian soldiers shoulder to shoulder. Within a few minutes, they became victims of the mines and the defensive fire.

94. The inflexibility of Russian methods of warfare was evidenced repeatedly, and could be illustrated by countless examples. Only the top Russian command during the last years of the war was an exception. This inflexibility manifested itself as high as army level; in divisions, regiments, and companies it was unquestionably the retarding factor in the way they fought. A division boundary was a sacred wall, and a neighbor's interest halted at his side of that wall. The senseless repetition of attacks, the rigidity of artillery fire, the plotting of lanes of attack

and movement without regard to terrain, all these were additional symptoms of this inflexibility. The oft-intercepted, frantic query, "The enemy has broken through! What shall we do?", was characteristic. Only a few subordinate commanders knew how to help themselves when the situation presented them with surprises of that nature. The leaders displayed a certain flexibility in their frequent shifting of units in the front lines. These units disappeared unnoticed overnight and reappeared several days later in another sector of the front. It was, however, no trick to relieve and exchange troops so long as one had the number of reserves that the Russians had; on the other hand, it was all the more difficult if one had none, as was the case with the Germans. The Russians have this method to thank for the fact that only a few of their units became thoroughly depleted during the course of prolonged battles; on the German side such a depletion became inevitable over the years of continuous service of units. None of the Soviet units that were thus shifted from sector to sector ever disappeared. It could be safely assumed that the unit withdrawn would be recommitted within the same army sector. The organization of an army, and the assignment of individual divisions to it also remained fixed. It seldom happened that divisions were interchanged between the armies.

   95. Though he was generally no master of improvisation, the Russian nevertheless knew how to bring battered infantry units up to strength, or how to constitute new units as replacements for destroyed ones. This procedure frequently was accomplished with startling speed, but it soon turned out to be an unscrupulous game played with human

lives. For example, the inhabitants of a threatened city, or perhaps the entire male population of areas from which we had recently withdrawn, were gathered up like lightning by means of excellent organization. Regardless of age, nationality, deferred status, or fitness, they were used to fill out these units. With no training at all, or, at most, only a few days of it, and often without weapons and uniforms, these soldiers were thrown into battle. They were supposed to learn in combat all that was necessary, and to acquire their weapons from their dead comrades. The Russians themselves were aware of the fact that these men were no soldiers, but they filled gaps and supplemented the sinking numbers of the "human mass." During the fighting in a bridgehead southeast of Kremenchug in September 1943, the Russians at nighttime used to drive ahead of their armed soldiers large numbers of civilians whom they had gathered up, so that the German infantry might expend its scant supply of ammunition.

96. The same old story again and again: employment of masses, and narrow division sectors held by large complements replenished time after time after time. Therefore also the mass attacks. In the twinkling of an eye the terrain in front of our line teemed with Russian soldiers. They seemed to grow out of the earth, and nothing would stop their advance for a while. Gaps closed automatically, and the mass surged on until the supply of men was used up and the wave, substantially thinned, receded again. How often we witnessed this typical picture of a Russian attack! It is impressive and astonding, on the other hand, how frequently the mass failed to recede, but rolled on and on, nothing able to stop it.

Repulsing such an attack was certainly dependent on the strength of our own forces and means for defense; primarily, however, it was a question of nerves. Only seasoned soldiers mastered the fear which instinctively gripped everyone upon the onslaught of such masses. Only the true soldier, the experienced individual fighter, could in the long run stand up under the strain; only a multitude of them could stop those masses.

97. Another specifically Russian battle technique was _infiltration_. It was a practice which especially suited the Russian, and of which he was a master. Despite closest observation of the avenues of approach, the Russian was suddenly there; no one knew where he had come from, nor how long he had already been there. Wherever the terrain was considered impassable, but was still kept under close observation to be doubly safe--just at those very points did the Russian infiltrate. He was suddenly there in substantial numbers and had already vanished into the earth. Nobody had seen a thing. What with the drawn-out German defense fronts, it was no particular art to steal between the widely separated strong points. Just the same, it was always a surprise when, despite all watchfulness during the night, we found the next morning that strong Russian units fully equipped with weapons and ammunition had assembled and dug in far behind our own front. These operations were executed with unbelievable skill, completely noiseless and almost always without a struggle. It was a very profitable technique which succeeded in hundreds of cases and gained the Russians great advantages. There was only one method of countering it: extreme watch-

fulness, and heavily occupied, deep positions, secured throughout at all times.

98. Of the same nature was the Russian's constant effort to establish bridgeheads (or advance covering positions, which are here included in the same category). These bridgeheads were to serve often to harass the German enemy and to sap his strength, and often as a base for Russian attacks. They were established by means of infiltration or by attack, and were a dangerous Russian tactic. It always proved wrong and absolutely hopeless to do nothing about those bridgeheads for the time being for this or that reason, and to postpone their elimination. It was dead certain that Russian bridgeheads which had existed only 24 hours would during that time have grown into a serious menace. Though only one Russian company might have occupied the newly formed bridgehead in the evening, by the next morning it was sure to have turned into an almost invincible fortress held by at least a regiment and bristling with heavy weapons. No mater how heavy and accurate our fire, the flow of men into the bridgehead continued. Regardless of all countermeasures the bridgehead continued to swell until it ran over. Only by using very strong forces and planned attack could it still be contained or eliminated, provided one was lucky and not afraid of heavy losses. Therefore, the warning against these bridgeheads can never be stressed sufficiently. There was only one way of fighting them, and that had to be made a rule: Every Russian bridgehead in the process of being formed, and every advanced position, no matter how small, must be attacked immediately, while it is still undeveloped, and eliminated. If we waited

even a few hours, we were in most cases too late, and on the next day success was more remote than ever. Even if there were but one platoon of infantry and one tank available, they had to be committed at once; the Russian was not yet dug in, he was still visible and within reach, he still had no organized defensive fire and no heavy weapons in the new position--a little later he had all of these. Every delay brought disaster; only an immediate counterattack led to success.

99. The Russian's kinship with nature expressed itself also in his preference for <u>night operations</u>. Shifts from one position to another, and concentrations, executed rapidly and silently in darkness, were more frequent than night attacks, which themselves were no rarity. However, the Russian generally avoided large-scale night attacks, since it appeared to him that the individual soldiers and subordinate commanders lacked the necessary self-reliance. A <u>major offensive operation</u> was conducted at night only when a victory definitely expected by the highest command had not been achieved in the course of daylight attacks. Such large-scale night attacks were mostly acts of desperation that failed to produce success. (See Example 20; and MS # T-36, Example (Beispiel) 33.) On the other hand, night attacks with a <u>limited objective</u> were a method which the Russians liked to employ in order to gain advantages for the next day, or to recapture lost ground. These night attacks were mostly infantry battles only, without use of artillery. It was always proper to be prepared for a Russian attempt to regain in the night a position that had been lost during the day.

100. The Russian's excellent <u>utilization of railroads</u>

should be noted here, even though it does not actually fall into the category of combat. The Russians accomplished strategic concentrations or shifts of large units, one or more armies, in an unbelievably short time with the help of the railroads. The imperfect rail net of European Russia did not often present opportunity for such measures, but wherever a chance offered itself, it was thoroughly utilized. Every expedient was used even though it bore the unmistakable mark of improvisation: a continuous succession of trains without any technical railroad safety measures; trains traveling one within sight of the next, or on two tracks in the same direction; reckless overcrowding and overloading of trains. The number of trains necessary per unit was less here than for any other army. The Russian neither had nor needed baggage or accessories, bulky clerk's lockers, surplus vehicles, or large food supplies. He could be packed into railroad cars like a sardine in a can. The wider gauge and the corresponding greater width of the Russian railroad car was significant in this respect. In any event, by using this type of railroad transport the Russians succeeded in surprising the German command, since such rapidity in large-scale troop movements by railroad contradicted all experience. (See rapid movement and intervention of the Siberian units in the battle of Moscow; MS # T-36, Example 22.)

101. Fighting the Russian on his own ground necessitated orientation in a new type of combat. Fighting had to be primitive and unscrupulous, but rapid and flexible. One could never afford to be nonplussed, not even in the face of the most surprising occurrences and

unexpected turns of events. Russian reactions to the tactical rules of warfare, and to tricks of the trade such as envelopment, flanking threat, feint, surprise, etc., could never be determined beforehand. One time the Russian would react according to the rules and give up sooner than anticipated; on another occasion, all efforts were to no avail, and neither encirclement nor flank attack fazed him. The struggle with the Russians was thereby placed on an entirely new basis; predictive calculation was out of the picture, and every action was full of suspense and surprise. At times, positions which were tactically decisive according to normal concepts would be evacuated by the Russians without delay. At other times, individual terrain features of no evident importance would be held even in the face of serious losses. In those instances the Russian often relied only on his intuition, which he substituted for his practical schooling. It must be conceded that this tactical instinct often stood the Russians in better stead than the theories of many academies could have done. The soundness of many an action which at first seemed surprising to us, often had to be recognized at a later time.

102. There was just one <u>tactical misconception</u> which the Russians could not relinquish despite all losses: the belief that an elevation was in every case the only terrain feature of value. They tried for every elevation, fought for it with perseverance and strong forces, no matter whether or not it actually dominated the terrain and the situation demanded its possession. If the elevation was really important, it was well to occupy it before the Russians; otherwise, it

was to be expected that the elevation could be taken only with heavy losses. In more cases than had earlier been assumed, however, the possession of level ground was sufficient; the value of the elevation was frequently overestimated.

103. Thus the Russian soldier voided a number of tactical principles. Still others were altered because of the nature of the country itself, a factor discussed in the following chapter.

Chapter Six

RUSSIA AS A THEATER OF OPERATIONS

104. The characteristics of Russian terrain brought about an inordinate number of new experiences, and created new doctrines of combat. Land and climate constituted weapons with which one had to be thoroughly familiar in order to deal with them, or, at least, to neutralize their restrictive effect. Their qualities altered tactical procedures formerly in common use, and forced the adoption of measures necessary for military operations in that particular area and climate.

105. In many instances, climate and soil conditions in the U. S. S. R. would for extended periods void all rules governing military movement. The German Army was not modern enough to overcome these difficulties, and therefore was forced to fight in winter and during muddy periods as best it could without the assistance of operative motor vehicles. This retrogression of about a century was a problem which could be dealt with only by means of improvisation. (See MSS # T-21 and T-36.)

106. The great forest and swamp areas of Arctic, Northern, and Central Russia often forced all movement into the narrow lanes of a few sand and swamp roads, and made it extremely difficult and time-consuming. Development of the columns was generally out of the question. The execution of any and all measures required a multiple of the usual

amount of time, and the advantage of motorization was almost negligible.

107. Sand, mud, and snow impeded the advance of all types of troops, and put great strain on motors. Lined up and jammed along one road, the troops slowly and painfully inched forward; a long snake crawling slowly over the difficult ground. The halt of one part of this snake stopped all parts behind it, pressing them still closer together. Weak bridges barely supported the infantry vehicles. Time-consuming bridge and road repairs were necessary, and many defiles had to be traversed. Previous experiences and doctrines were useless under these conditions. Time calculations, the most important factor in operations, had to be based on entirely new concepts. Frequently the time required for a movement could not be estimated even approximately. It continued to run far in excess of the expected maximum. (See MS # T-36, Example 4.) Remedies were difficult and could be achieved only by flexibility and practice.

108. In by far the largest part of Southern Russia, and in most of the swampless areas of Northern and Central Russia, travel in dry weather was considerably better, and the terrain, too, was passable for vehicles of all types almost everywhere. During that time, operations on even the largest scale were possible everywhere with the exception of swamp areas. (See MS # T-36, "Der Sommer")

109. The principle of establishing <u>lanes of movement</u> rather than routes of advance proved satisfactory on the German as well as on the Russian side; the same was true of the separation of lanes of movement for motorized and non-motorized units. Here the motorized troops

had to be allotted the lanes with the best roads. Engineers were always placed far up in the column so that they might quickly reinforce bridges and eliminate terrain obstacles. Only strict <u>regulation of traffic</u>, and relentlessly severe discipline, guaranteed the best possible progress. Every halt for rest had to be closely timed, passing procedure strictly regulated, and priority definitely determined. Each driver pressed forward, and in unguarded moments became a traffic violator. For that reason, trained troops were needed for traffic control, and had to be used, just as every tactical unit, according to the point of main effort. Likewise, all staffs and higher headquarters had to abide by traffic discipline, since exceptions only caused confusion. In particularly difficult large-scale movements, <u>special purpose staffs</u> under the command of senior officers were employed. (See MS # T-21, Example 69.)

110. The <u>rate of progress</u> of motorized troops could be roughly estimated in advance only if they were traveling on hard-surfaced roads. A <u>rule of thumb</u> is that, on average dry roadways, motorized troops can make from eight to ten kilometers per hour, and foot troops from two to four kilometers per hour. Reference information for rates of march under very difficult conditions may be found in several Examples in <u>Klimatische Bedingungen im Osten</u> (MS # T-36). Terrain and road conditions in the East required, according to our experience, <u>three to four times the amount of motor fuel</u> needed under normal European conditions.

111. The assumption that long columns can easily be stopped by the enemy appears justified. However, it developed that the Russian overestimated the <u>constraining effect</u> of the channeled movements. In

almost every case he blocked only the roads and bridges with task forces deployed without breadth or depth. It was, therefore, not too difficult to knock out such enemy blocking attempts by attacks against the flanks and rear of the enemy groups. This maneuver required two conditions for success: reconnaissance far to the front, and incorporation of combat forces capable of cross-country movement at the head of the march groups. No matter how easy it was for vehicles with cross-country mobility to cross great, open stretches in any direction during dry seasons, they nevertheless were confined mostly to the existing roads on long marches, since the Russian terrain always confronted them with terrain obstacles which they were unable to overcome (swamps, watercourses, ravines, steep rises, etc.). Furthermore, it required considerably more time and fuel to move cross-country.

112. MS # T-36 deals at length with the <u>serious difficulties</u> of movement and combat in Russia that arose <u>by virtue of climatic conditions</u>. That same manuscript, as well as <u>Improvisationen als Mittel der Fuehrung</u> (MS # T-21), also describes the numerous expedients that the German Army and the Luftwaffe had to resort to in order to surmount those difficulties. However, in drawing conclusions from the battles of the German armies in the East it is to be noted that the German Armed Forces went unprepared into the Russian winter and into the muddy periods, and for that reason they faced numerous difficulties and emergencies which could have been avoided by conscientious preparation.

PECULIARITIES
OF
RUSSIAN TACTICS

CONTENTS

	Page
Chapter One – GENERAL	63
Chapter Two – RECONNAISSANCE AND SECURITY	66
Chapter Three – OFFENSE	71
I. Winter the Preferred Season	71
II. The Employment of Mass	72
III. Development of Russian Offensive Tactics	79
IV. The Use of Armor	86
Chapter Four – DEFENSE	100
I. General	100
II. Use of Mines	104
III. Conduct of Battle	107
Chapter Five – RETREAT AND DELAYING ENGAGEMENTS	125
Chapter Six – COMBAT UNDER UNUSUAL CONDITIONS	127
I. Fighting in Towns and Villages	127
II. Forest Fighting	130

		Page
III.	Fighting Around Rivers, Swamps, and Lakes	137
IV.	Fighting in Darkness and Inclement Weather	141

Chapter Seven - CAMOUFLAGE, DECEPTION, AND PROPAGANDA 147

I.	Camouflage	147
II.	Deception	149
III.	Propaganda	151

Chapter One
GENERAL

113. Comprehension of Russian tactics demands a clear conception of the premises on which they are based. Russian tactics have their roots in the <u>Russian himself</u> and in his social order, in the <u>Russian land mass</u> with its climate and soil conditions, its expanse, and its varied topography. The most important points on those subjects have been summed up elsewhere in this report, as well as in MSS # T-21 and T-36. These points will be supplemented in detail in the following pages, and illustrated by numerous examples. The examples should permit insight into the practical effect of these characteristics under various conditions, and illustrate how the German command coped with them.

114. While the bulk of the Red Army consisted of <u>infantry divisions</u>, which were combined into corps and armies, and supplemented by numerous GHQ troops (artillery, antitank, and engineer brigades, as well as tank and self-propelled artillery elements), there were also the large, highly mobile <u>tank and mechanized corps</u>--the strategic force --which in most instances were combined into tank armies. Tank corps and mechanized corps were seldom placed under infantry armies. This method of organization reveals the effort of the Russian high command to assure strategic mobility. That mobility was demonstrated in the sweeping employment of these large fast forces. As soon as the battle

fronts became static (position warfare), the Russian command withdrew its tank and mechanized forces from the front, and did not commit them again until the infantry had breached the enemy defensive system. That mode of employment coincided with the concepts expressed in the Russian field service regulations. In fighting for a system of defensive positions, GHQ tank and self-propelled artillery regiments (that is, not the organic forces of the mobile corps) supported the infantry divisions in great numbers.

115. Because of the long duration of the war it was possible to observe the combat methods of the Russian enemy in all phases. As early as the first winter in Russia, it was evident that the German lower command would have to find new methods of fighting if it wanted to be successful. The extensive area, the mass employment of men, the peculiar characteristics of Russian fighting methods, and the different climatic conditions forced them to develop a new line of tactical thought. Only a better-led soldier, and one superior in fighting qualities, had any prospect of success. In logical sequence, those thoughts had to concern close observation of all Russian habits, Russian reaction to German fighting methods, and thorough exploitation of Russian weaknesses. In order to make information about the characteristics of the Russian available to all concerned, it was exceedingly important to compile all experiences and to disseminate them, particularly to the replacement training units and to the schools. There had to be a constant flow of instructors with combat experience to these units in order to train replacements and new recruits according to the latest

experiences.

116. These measures proved invaluable. Divisions that had been newly formed, or transferred from other theaters, and sent to the East without a sufficient number of <u>officers and noncommissioned officers with prior experience in the East</u>, failed in the beginning almost without exception and suffered heavy losses. On the other hand, even remnants of divisions which had long been going through the hard school of the East, made outstanding accomplishments (see Examples in MSS # T-36 and T-21). At the same time, divisions which had fought in the East performed excellently also on all other fronts.

Chapter Two

RECONNAISSANCE AND SECURITY

117. Russian <u>march reconnaissance</u> and <u>security</u> generally corresponded to German concepts. There was no really intense activity, but one very skillfully adapted to the objective and to local conditions (terrain, climate, transportation routes, and weather).

118. In his march reconnaissance the Russian was very hesitant, groping, and cautious. He allowed himself much time. If he found no enemy resistance, he frequently plunged ahead into the unknown without further reconnaissance.

<u>Ex. 8</u> The Engagement at Maloryta (End of June 1941)

<u>App. 2</u> 119. The engagement at Maloryta grew out of the thrust of a Russian division east of the Bug near Wlodawa, into the flank of our armored units which were rolling from Brest-Litovsk through Kobryn in the direction of Slutsk. The Russian division had sent ahead armored reconnaissance cars. These made their appearance about half a day before the division itself, and encountered our 255th Infantry Division, which was advancing from Wlodawa on Maloryta. The terrain (Pripyat Marshes) was extremely unfavorable for armored reconnaissance cars. Nevertheless, they came on. After two cars had been knocked out, the others disappeared for good. Instead, there appeared after a few hours infantry security detachments, already deployed as a thin screen of skirmishers. Several kilometers behind followed the rifle division split into battle teams (Kampfgruppen), which were deployed over a front of about 10 kilometers, with large gaps between the teams.

The Russian division had undoubtedly anticipated an encounter with the Germans in the vicinity of Maloryta, and so had sent out motorized reconnaissance to obtain promptly the information needed for deployment for action of the division. The infantry screens following later served as local security for the battle teams.

Ex. 9   The Action Southeast of Plavskoye (November 1941)

120. The Russians intended to thrust from Yefremov along the main road to the northwest in the direction of Tula, into the rear of our armored units which were before Tula. When the leading elements of our 167th Infantry Division met them near Teploye, the Russians were just as surprised as we were. Certainly they had not yet counted on meeting the enemy. On this basis, their advance can be taken as typical of a Russian march against the enemy with only one usable road available, when direct contact with the enemy is not yet expected. Again, several armored reconnaissance cars appeared at first, but they seemed to have only local reconnaissance missions. They moved ahead by bounds. Behind them, following German procedure, came infantry security detachments. Only then followed the foremost division (6th Rifle Division). This division possessed numerous trucks, which, however, were not used until later during local shifts on the battlefield. They were not intended for the strategic forward displacement of the division at this time. On the road there followed behind the 6th Rifle Division further infantry divisions without such a great number of trucks. Several days later, when the battle was already in progress, there appeared a cavalry division which had come up on a bad side road running to the west. There also appeared a tank brigade, which had been standing ready behind the long column of rifle divisions. It was thrown forward in a single movement only when the battle had reached its climax.

121. It seemed as if in an advance against the enemy the chain of rifle divisions following one another was not to be disturbed. Accordingly, though it would have been possible to move a single division forward, this was not done. Perhaps this maneuver was also to serve the purpose of preventing the enemy from recognizing the movement prematurely. Had the cavalry division advanced simultaneously with the rifle divisions, the Russians would not have been able to surprise us.

122. For combat reconnaissance, the Russian used either assault teams in platoon strength, or tanks alone or in combination with riflemen.

Ex. 10
App. 3

123. The following example from the Kandalaksha front shows the use of stationary security detachments for the protection of a flanking movement.

> About one kilometer in front of our strong points in the no man's land of primeval forest north of the Arctic Circle there was a small range of hills, the Ahvenvaara. It was unoccupied most of the time, but now and then either we or the Russians would occupy it temporarily in order to use it as an anchor point for operations. One day in March 1944 this range of hills was again occupied by weak Russian forces. Assuming that the Russians would, as they had for years, leave again after a short time, we took no action. In a few days, however, a whole battalion had infiltrated, and it was too late for our few forces to dislodge them. In the same way, the Russians occupied an elevation farther to the west, where they drove off our weak security detachments and immediately set up a strong point. Under the protection of these two points, the Russians moved their attack troops into our northern front. This was an instance of planned, far-sighted preparation for moving attack troops into the jump-off position for a subsequent attack based on a stabilized front. The Russians were completely successful in their security measures for those movements.

124. The preceding three examples reveal that the Russian demonstrated great adaptibility in march reconnissance and security, and that he knew how to take proper action under diverse circumstances. In mobile warfare we observe the use of fast-working motorized reconnaissance on approaching an expected enemy, and as its result the developed advance of battle groups (Kampfgruppen) under cover of local infantry security detachments. In advancing upon an enemy with whom an engage-

ment is not anticipated in the near future, we find the Russian employing an almost schematic local march-reconnaissance pattern: armored reconnaissance cars moving ahead in rapid bounds, and behind them normal infantry march security. There also seems to be a definite effort to hold the forces together and to prevent ventures on the part of individual elements. Further, in a kind of position warfare—even in primeval forest wilderness—we observe first the methodical establishment of firm strong points, under the protection of which the march movements of the units destined to attack are subsequently to be executed. Surprise attacks into the Russian march movement—in the example presented, such surprise attacks would have meant a flanking march of almost sixty kilometers—are thereby to be eliminated.

125. On stablized fronts, the Russian conducted his reconnaissance with patrols, or by reconnaissance in force. He was exceedingly adept at combat reconnaissance in offensive as well as in defensive operations. He knew how to adapt his reconnaissance patrols to the terrain and how to employ them in great numbers. Seldom could any conclusion as to the intentions of the Russian enemy be drawn from his reconnaissance-patrol activity.

126. For <u>reconnaissance in force</u>, the Russian employed forces at least in company strength, but frequently also in battalion and regimental strength. They were supported in their operations by concentrated artillery fire, and often by accompanying tanks as well. The main objective of such attacks was the taking of prisoners, and sometimes the capture of an important terrain feature.

127. Another frequently employed Russian method of reconnaissance was the <u>ambush</u> of our reconnaissance patrols. The Russian was a master at this procedure. Well camouflaged, he could lie in wait for hours until the opportunity presented itself. He also knew how to sneak up and surprise isolated outguards. The employment of dogs trained in tracking ambush patrols proved a satisfactory countermeasure.

128. The Russians also made considerable use of the <u>civilian population</u> for intelligence missions, using them to obtain the desired reports on the enemy situation. A pet practice was the employment of <u>boys eight to fourteen years old</u>. They were first trained for this work and then allowed to infiltrate at suitable front sectors.

<u>Ex. 11</u> 129. Before the offensive (Operation ZITADELLE) in July 1943, for example, more than a dozen such children were picked up in the Byelgorod sector alone. They gave detailed reports on the kind of training they received and on their modus operandi. The training of the children we picked up had been supervised by Russian officers. It had lasted four weeks, and there had been sixty participants. The youths came from communities near the front on both sides of the battle lines, and therefore were thoroughly familiar with the locale. Many were staying with relatives or acquaintances in German-occupied localities, and were therefore not easy to discover and apprehend. Their talent for observation and their skill at spying were remarkable. For this reason, civilians in localities near the front (six to ten kilometers behind the front line) had to be evacuated not only because of the danger from enemy fire, but also as a preventive measure against espionage.

Chapter Three

OFFENSE

The national characteristics, which have already been described, and the peculiarities of the country were the principal factors determining the Russian conduct of battle.

I. <u>Winter the Preferred Season</u>

130. The Russians preferred to carry out their major offensives in winter, because their troops were accustomed to that season, and very well equipped and trained for it. The Russians were superior to all peoples of Central and Western Europe in enduring rigors of weather and climate. Casualties from the cold were an exception in their army. Soldiers with frostbite were severely punished. Even in the harsh winter of 1941-42 the Russians were able to spend many days in the snow, protected only by simple windbreaks, without detriment to their health.

<u>Ex. 12</u> 131. In the winter of 1941-42, from 6 December 1941 to 14 April 1942, the Soviets carried out their first major offensive in the area west of Moscow. They penetrated to the Vyazma--Rzhev line. In their large-scale attack from the Stalingrad--Don area the Russians succeeded in encircling the German Sixth Army at Stalingrad, and in overrunning the front of the German allies. In the period from 19 November 1942 to the middle of March 1943 they succeeded in creating a fluid situation along a 1,500-kilometer stretch of the Eastern Front, and in penetrating up to 500

kilometers toward the west.

On Christmas of 1943 there began the Russian offensive from the area southwest of Kiev. It continued until the thaw period in March 1944 and led to the annihilation of German divisions in the Cherkassy pocket, the encirclement of Tarnopol and of the German First Panzer Army, and the retrograde correction of the German front to a line east of Stanislav--Lwow--Kowel.

The Russian general offensive began along the entire Eastern Front in mid-January of 1945. It led to the loss of Hungary, Poland, Silesia, East Prussia, and Pomerania. After short local halts, the Russians stood before Vienna and Berlin, and in co-operation with the armed forces of the Western Powers brought about the end of the war.

II. The Employment of Mass

Only the use of masses of men and equipment enabled the Russians to accomplish these great feats.

132. Even in World War I the so-called steam roller was the core of the Russian system of attack. At that time, however, it was limited to the employment of the human mass. For that reason its initial successes were paid for by myriads of human lives. Later, undermined politically from within, it broke up and finally disintegrated. That sealed the doom of the Russian Imperial Army.

133. The surprise start of the Eastern Campaign in World War II at first prevented the forming of a Russian steam roller. For that reason the beginning of the war was marked by a Soviet reverse. Relying, however, on inexhaustible reserves and the rigors of his boundless territory, the Russian brought up his human masses and created anew the famous steam roller. Strengthened by a mass of equipment and welded to-

MS # T-22   -73-

gether by the caresses and whiplashes of Communism, it became invincible in spite of numerous setbacks. Step by step the German Army was pounded to pieces and crushed as it succumbed to what might be termed the modern <u>super steam roller</u>.

134. <u>Infiltration</u> was an expedient which was made possible by the vastness of the Russian territory, and which was primarily used where masses were not available or could not be employed.

135. As early as 1941 the Russians made repeated attempts to check the German offensive by <u>counterattacks</u>. To this end they opposed it with cavalry and tank forces, and sometimes with masses of infantry. They succeeded in checking the German Army locally and temporarily, but were unsuccessful in stopping the great offensive as a whole. The following examples illustrate the Russian type of attack at that time.

<u>Ex. 13</u>   <u>The Battle in the Dnepr--Beresina Triangle (Mid-July to Mid-August 1941)</u>
<u>App. 4</u>

136. The battle in the Dnepr--Beresina triangle resulted from Timoshenko's plan to envelop in a pincers movement both flanks of the German armored units which had advanced across the Dnepr, and to cut them off from the rear. Since the northern arm of this pincers had already been destroyed near Orsha, and LIII Infantry Corps already had almost made connection with the armored units on the Dnepr by a rapid advance via Slutsk--Bobruisk, a battle developed not between Timoshenko and the armored units, but between the Russians and LIII Infantry Corps, which was taking over the protection of the flanks and rear of the second armored unit.

137. The attack was very carefully prepared. As early as February 1941, during a conference near Bobruisk, Timoshenko had discussed this operation in a kind of

map exercise with his higher commanders. In order to put it into effect, three divisions located in the vicinity of Kiev were transferred to the neighborhood of Gomel immediately after the outbreak of hostilities. Here, they were excellently concealed and kept in readiness until the time for action came. The Moscow School of Artillery was called upon. By means of prisoners, 53 different rifle regiments were identified during the course of battle; some of them had even come from the Caucasus. In order to take immediate advantage of the expected success, a detachment of specialists from Moscow very quickly repaired the railroad bridge over the Dnepr at Zhlobin during the course of the battle. The bridge had been blown up prematurely when our armored units approached the town. Timoshenko reopened the bridge in person. Thus, all preparations seemed to have been made to ensure the success of the operation and to exploit it. The higher command had, even according to our standards, done as much as could be expected.

138. Tactical measures during the first stage of the battle were entirely appropriate. Our 4th Panzer Division, which had crossed the Dnepr near Rogachev, was thrown back across the river. Simultaneously with the withdrawing armored vehicles, the Russians crossed the Dnepr in close pursuit, and for the time being there was nothing to stop their advance, since the armor turned off to the north. At Zhlobin, where there were only weak armored security forces, they faced practically no opposition at all. The Russians did not take advantage of this favorable situation. They moved forward very slowly, so that very small, hastily motorized forces of the 255th and 267th Infantry Divisions could be thrown against them. These German forces held the Russians at bay until the divisions themselves arrived after a day or two. Thus it happened that the Russians pushed only ten kilometers to the west of the Dnepr both at Zhlobin and Rogachev. One might almost think that this was the area that had been planned as the first day's objective in Timoshenko's war game. More territory could unquestionably have been taken, had the advance been conducted more energetically. The passing up of this opportunity, however, is to be attributed to the intermediate command. By the time the higher command learned of the situation, it was too late. The subsequent Russian attacks were carried out in the form of outflanking and enveloping movements while pinning down our front. They occasioned

many a critical situation. However, when our greatest worry had been eliminated after the commitment of the 55th Infantry Division, and our front began to be more stabilized, the Russian command exhausted itself by repeated attacks on the same points. The Russians failed to recognize the fact that the opposing forces were now of equal strength, and that therefore nothing more was to be achieved by the battle.

139. It soon became evident, however, that the strategic situation of the Russians was becoming steadily less tenable. The advance of XII Infantry Corps northeast of Rogachev, and of XLIII Infantry Corps to the lower Beresina made the grave danger facing the Russians unmistakably clear. Nevertheless, they held firmly to the originally planned thrust, even when it was high time to escape envelopment. This led to the Gomel pocket and the annihilation of the Russian main attack army. That catastrophe could have been avoided, had the Russian command drawn its conclusions from the situation in time.

Ex. 14

App. 5

Fighting in the Poretsye Bridgehead on the Luga (Mid-July to August 1941)

140. As stated in MS # T-36, Example 4, a strong combat element of the 6th Panzer Division succeeded in effecting a surprise capture of the two Luga bridges at Poretsye (105 kilometers southwest of Leningrad) on 14 July 1941, and in forming a bridgehead. The strong armored forces which followed, remained stuck for days in swampy forests. Therefore, the force (Kampfgruppe) was for a long time entirely on its own. Three alerted proletarian divisions and armored units from Leningrad were dispatched to the Luga by rail and motor vehicles, with the mission of annihilating the German forces.

141. Nevertheless, the German force, consisting of only two infantry battalions, one panzer battalion, two artillery battalions, one Flak battalion, and a company of engineers, was able to stand its ground against an enemy six times as strong, despite the fact that it could no longer be reached and supported by our aircraft. The bridgehead was almost four kilometers deep, but only four hundred meters wide, and was completely surrounded by swampy forests which could be traversed in summer by infantry. The enemy, however, had no visibility, because the edges of the woods were in our hands. Enemy

artillery fired twenty times as many rounds per day as our own batteries. It pounded the bridges and the edges of the woods. In unobserved fire the enemy sent more than two thousand medium shells a day in the direction of the bridges without ever hitting them. Enemy aircraft roared all day above the narrow corridor of the bridgehead and inflicted serious losses on our troops. Soon, therefore, the road was lined with a long row of German soldiers' graves, marked with birchwood crosses. As often as ten times a day the enemy attacked the road fork which was enclosed by the projecting arc of the bridgehead. Each attack was headed by as many tanks, echeloned in depth, as the narrow road would accommodate. Time and again the enemy attacks were repulsed, and time and again they were renewed. Wave after wave of Russian forces assembled, concealed by many wrecked tanks and heaps of corpses, and stormed recklessly into the murderous defensive fire. The attacks did not subside until the enemy no longer had the necessary men and ammunition at his disposal. Soon, however, replacements of proletarians and new ammunition supplies arrived from Leningrad. The assaults on the road fork were stubbornly and incessantly resumed until passage through the narrow attack corridors was no longer possible because they were completely clogged by disabled enemy tanks and decaying heaps of corpses. Later, we counted more than 2,000 dead Russians and 78 knocked-out enemy tanks in this narrow combat zone alone.

142. The only variation, which was itself invariant, consisted of enemy attacks sometimes along both sides of the road leading to the fork from the north, and at other times on the road coming from the south. A simultaneous attack from both sides never took place, however, for different divisions were involved which did not co-ordinate their attacks. The tanks always attacked along the northern road. Their attacks, too, ceased only when it was no longer possible to pass between the 78 wrecks. The swampy forests and a reservoir fifteen meters deep prevented a by-passing of that obstacle.

143. The following attacks were aimed at cutting off the bridgehead and were conducted through the woods. It was impossible to prevent the mass assaults, since the long flanks of the narrow bridgehead could be manned with only a small number of forces. The attacks were expected and the defense arranged accord-

MS # T-22   -77-

ingly. Two tank units, held in readiness one at the road fork and one at the bridges, and reinforced by armored infantry companies, had orders in case of an enemy break-through to the road to attack the enemy immediately from both sides and to annihilate him. This flexible fighting method proved itself well. With the same stubbornness he had formerly shown in attacking the road fork, the enemy now made several assaults daily on the flanks, and each time succeeded in reaching the road. Within a scant half-hour he would be attacked from both sides and destroyed by tank fire. Only remnants succeeded in escaping through the woods. Not until the attempt to cut off the group failed with severe losses just as often as it was undertaken, did the enemy give up this procedure and attack the bridges directly. In this way a 150-man enemy battalion succeeded in reaching the southern bridge after overcoming its weak defenses. While the enemy forces were crossing the bridge, German armored personnel carriers took them by surprise and destroyed them to the last man. Contrary to his usual custom, the enemy did not repeat this venture. Instead, he sent a reinforced infantry regiment from Kingisepp, and later two battalions of the 3d Proletarian Division, against the rear of the bridgehead. Both operations were caught in a pincers movement between the leading elements of the main forces, which had been stalled and were now approaching from the southwest, and a reinforced armored unit of the bridgehead coming from the opposite direction. The enemy regiment was scattered and the two battalions were destroyed. The bridgehead was then strengthened by forces coming up from the rear, and became impregnable.

144. This example demonstrates the complete failure of the intermediate and lower Russian commands, who did not understand how to co-ordinate the different units and weapons into a common, simultaneous attack from all sides. The weak German units, which were fighting a losing battle, would not have been able to withstand such an attack.

Ex. 15   The Meeting Engagement near Plavskoye (November 1941)

App. 6   145. The Russian attacks in the battle southeast of Plavskoye in November 1941 developed from a pure meeting engagement. The Russian forces, which were to advance against our armored forces before Tula, suddenly faced LIII

Infantry Corps coming from the west. The Russian command adapted itself skillfully to the new situation. The situation was made easier on both sides by the fact that the points met first, and that each opponent was then able to deploy its forces from depth. It was, therefore, several days before the battle mounted to a climax once the long columns had been deployed on both sides.

146. Strategically, the Russian thrust on Tula was well planned. At this stage the Russian higher command also acted correctly from a tactical standpoint, and the Russian 6th Rifle Division, which bore the initial brunt of the battle, was tactically well commanded. Under the completely unclarified conditions, the Russian higher command apparently wanted to avoid having its foremost division repulsed, and so brought it to a halt. The division, deployed laterally, blocked the advance of the first German regiment to appear. In addition, the Russian higher command attempted to bring up for the anticipated battle all forces available in the vicinity. The Russian cavalry division, which had advanced north of the combat area, abandoned its operations against the 112th Infantry Division and appeared on the scene. Furthermore, a cavalry division located near Yefremov was ordered forward over side roads past the march columns of the Russian rifle division, in order to cut the Orel--Plavskoye road in the neighborhood of Chern. In this connection there ensued a sharp clash between the commander of the Bryansk Army Group in Yelets, who was in command here, and the commander of this cavalry division. According to captured documents, the following happened: The Army Group Commander ordered the cavalry division to proceed by a forced march to the Orel--Tula road, a distance of sixty kilometers. The cavalry division commander made a written reply stating that this was impossible, because 20 percent of his horses were completely unshod, and of the remaining horses 80 percent had no hind shoes, and 20 percent no fore shoes. For that reason the division was unfit to move. Thereupon the higher commander repeated the order for the forced march in no uncertain terms. The cavalry division started out, but actually went only forty kilometers. It had then reached the end of its tether. At any rate, it had effected a connection with the front and extended it. The iron determination of the Army Group Commander had not achieved the desired success, but nevertheless it had created new difficulties for us.

MS # T-22

147. The 6th Rifle Division was very mobile in its fighting. When its western flank was threatened and the divisions following it had not yet come up, it withdrew far enough by using its numerous trucks so that the threat to its flank was eliminated. It did not move forward again until the next division could be turned against the threat to its flank. The other divisions were employed according to the prevailing situation and by forming very concentrated points of main effort. They attacked by deploying directly from march columns, without going into assembly positions. Not until they were all disposed along the battle front was the tank brigade, which had been far to the rear, committed in order to strike the decisive blow against whatever seemed to be our weakest spot. This was on about the fifth day of battle. Only rapid shifting of our own forces prevented an enemy success.

148. To be sure, when LIII Infantry Corps subsequently launched its attack, the Rifle Division, which had become immobile to a great extent, was wiped out. The westernmost cavalry division had already been eliminated. However, the bulk of the enemy forces escaped annihilation by hasty withdrawal, sacrificing much of their equipment. This was the first instance in the Corps' experience that the higher Russian command withdrew from a situation that was beginning to take an unfavorable turn, instead of sticking it out. The intervention of LIII Infantry Corps, in any event, upset the Russian large-scale plan of operations from the very start. The attempt to force a way to Tula in spite of this had failed. The Russian higher command now actually drew the proper inferences from the situation. They adopted new methods.

III. Development of Russian Offensive Tactics

149. The Russians carried out their first large-scale offensive that followed a preconceived plan in the severe winter of 1941-42 in the Moscow area. It was well thought out, and cleverly exploited the severe detrimental effect which the muddy period and the onset of the cold season had on the striking power of the German Army, unprepared as it was

for winter warfare. (See captured order of the Russian High Command, MS # T-36, Example 21.) This offensive did mark the turning point in the Eastern Campaign; it did not, however, decide it, as the Russians had expected it to do. Therefore, it did not achieve the intended purpose.

150. The fighting methods of the Russian troops are revealed in the Examples of winter warfare during 1941-42 contained in MS # T-36. The <u>mass attack</u> was supposed to shatter and break up the German front. Units penetrating and infiltrating through the lines were to cut off the supply lines.

151. The German front was not yet ready for defense when frost set in. Some sectors were still fluid. The solidly frozen ground and the exceedingly heavy snowfalls precluded the methodical construction of a defensive position. Taking advantage of the dusky weather and the blizzards, the first waves of Russians, clad in white camouflage coats, worked their way close to the German positions without being detected. Wave after wave, driven on by the commissars, surged against the German lines. At that time the Russians knew nothing as yet about methodical preparation for an attack by means of concentrated fire of heavy weapons and artillery, or by the employment of massed tanks.

152. When the attacks continually failed and enormous losses were incurred, the Russians changed over to <u>infiltration tactics</u>. Forces capable of rapid movement were generally used for this purpose. Tanks and ski units were preferred when the terrain permitted their use.

Except for a few local reconnaissance thrusts, the Russians regularly attacked on a broad front. They always assembled far superior forces for those attacks. Co-operation between the different arms of the service improved noticeably. It was patterned after German offensive tactics. Russian methods of attack were subjected to many changes as a result of war experiences. In 1941-42 the Russians always resorted to mass attacks after bringing up strong reserves. Thus, for example, they repeated their attacks against the Fourth Army for weeks at a time in the same place during the so-called Battles of the Rollbahn* near Smolensk be-

----
*Ed: Express motor highway, in this case the Minsk--Moscow road.
----

tween 21 October and 4 December. Co-operation between the various infantry weapons likewise was imperfect. Attacks on German unit boundaries, which the Russians always sought and usually detected, were dangerous. Artillery support was active, but as yet often without a definite fire plan.

153. The year 1943 brought a definite change in the method of attack. Concentrated artillery fires were employed more frequently and supplemented by massed mortar attacks. The Russians tried to infiltrate through known German weak points. For this purpose they preferred forest areas or hollows previously designated by the tactical command. If they succeeded in infiltrating by this system, they immediately entrenched themselves and laid mines. Subsequently, a period of vulnerability set in, because the bringing up of the artillery and heavy weapons proceeded very slowly, and co-operation with them ceased

abruptly.

154. The <u>employment of massed tanks</u> brought about a revolutionary change in Russian tactics in 1944. After a drum fire of artillery, a large number of tanks went over to the attack, followed by the infantry in deep wedges. While the artillery gave good support at first, communications with it frequently broke off during a further advance. To the very end of the war it was difficult for the Russians to co-ordinate fire and movement. The penetrations were deep, and invariably in a straight line. Then a halt was called in order to bring up the greatest possible number of infantry during the night. These masses of infantry dug in as soon as they caught up with the points of the attack. The assault wedges were brought up in echelons behind the tanks.

155. Since the German counterattacks were usually launched when the enemy infantry was separated from its tanks, the Russians began in 1945 to make deep thrusts with infantry riding on tanks. These thrusts often went so deep that contact with the main forces was lost. The Russians were able to take that risk because the German front of 1945 had been bled white and no longer had adequate reserves available to destroy those far-advanced, strong enemy forces.

156. The fact that the Russians built <u>field fortifications</u> never meant that they had no plans of attacking. The Russian always dug in. The time for being suspicious came only when a gradual <u>sapping toward our lines</u> into a jump-off position for an assault could be noted in connection with his entrenchment activities. That usually

meant preparation for attack. Recognized preparations behind a front sector did not necessarily indicate that he would attack at the particular point. He launched surprise attacks by skillfully and quickly shifting his attack forces to the planned assembly area during the course of one night. Numerous reconnaissance thrusts, supported by artillery and tanks, and conducted on a broad front both by day and night in strength up to a regiment, were to procure information for an attack and to confuse or deceive the enemy as to the time and place of the attack. Movement behind the front, even at night, was not necessarily followed by an attack. The Soviets were very skillful in the use of feints, sham installations, and dummies of all types. Evaluation of artillery observation data, often painstakingly carried out for weeks, and constant interrogation of prisoners, whose statements were checked by our reconnaissance operations, produced reliable evidence of an impending attack. The enemy often cleverly concealed a projected assembly of his artillery by means of extraordinary emplacement activity and by a highly mobile employment of roving guns and batteries. He was also very cautious about trial fire whenever it was not executed for purposes of deception.

157. Not until later did the Russians make extensive use, in the attack, of artillery fire based on mathematical computation. Despite all their efforts at concealing their true intentions, however, the pattern of enemy artillery activity, carefully worked out day by day, still revealed very reliable clues as to impending enemy attacks. One could often observe that a few days before an attack the Russian

moved about as little as possible by day or night, and that his combat activity decreased noticeably, until suddenly the attack was launched out of a clear sky.

158. <u>Secondary attacks and feints</u> were often launched at the same time as the main attack in order to make the assault front appear as broad as possible, and at the same time cause the enemy to split up his defense forces. In the summer of 1943, the Russians used <u>smoke</u> on a broad front while carrying out attacks across the Donets, in order to conceal preparations and to deny observation to the Germans. At that time the Russians incurred severe losses. The XXX Infantry Corps repulsed all attacks and attempts to cross the Donets by immediately concentrating the fire of all heavy weapons straight into the smoke. At that time the Russians still were very inexperienced in the use of smoke and did not make use of dummy smoke screens. Likewise, they failed to understand the principle of laying a smoke screen over German observers in order to blind them. At that time, too, the Russians did not necessarily carry out their attacks with artillery preparation. When they did, their artillery, massed into points of main effort, laid a <u>rigid concentration</u> on infantry positions, battery positions, towns, and road junctions. During the artillery preparation the infantry worked its way forward into the jump-off position by a process of infiltration, and from that point made a mass advance. When the first objective, which was still within range of the supporting artillery, was reached, a long halt set in, since the Russians were not in a position to displace their artillery and heavy weapons for-

ward in a manner that would allow a continuous forward thrust. The infantry immediately dug in and felt its way forward only by means of combat reconnaissance. During the halts, the infantry had to rely almost exclusively on local support from accompanying tanks and mortars. The Russian heavy <u>mortar battalions</u> (<u>Ed</u>: Probably 120-mm.) were an ideal direct-support artillery for infantry. However, they also were too slow for continuous support of the infantry in an attack. The <u>infantry-support tanks</u> acted very cautiously and fought more in the manner of self-propelled assault guns, like armored artillery pieces of the infantry.

159. Even at the beginning of the Campaign the enemy infantry were very clever at utilizing terrain features. If the Russians could not continue their current main attacks with the desired success by day, they proceeded to launch local attacks during the night. In that case, they either launched sudden mass attacks, or infiltrated at many points through our lines, which for the most part were lightly manned. Thus, in a night attack on the 97th Light Infantry Division in the winter of 1941, they broke through our lines east of Artemovsk in the Donets Basin with an entire cavalry division. However, the next day this division was cut down to the last man.

160. Also in the battle of encirclement at Uman in 1941, and at Beli--southeast of Toropets--in November 1942, thousands of Russian soldiers without equipment or heavy weapons penetrated our thin lines during hours of darkness by piecemeal infiltration. Well-prepared night attacks were rare.

161. The low-flying aircraft supporting the main efforts picked as their principal targets the defending infantry, batteries, reserves, supplies, and villages in the divisional combat sectors. The attack planes did not venture far into the rear area.

162. In order to develop the war of position into mobile warfare later in the Eastern Campaign, the Red Army command concentrated its forces, which were numerically far superior to those of the Germans, into more and more powerful masses at the points of main effort and, after heavy artillery concentrations, broke through or sent the German front reeling. The Russian command attempted to conceal strategic preparations for large-scale attacks from our reconnaissance, and therefore carried them out only at night. Preparations could thus be detected only by night aerial reconnaissance. Night truck transport operations on a grand scale (2,000 to 3,000 trucks in each direction in the course of one night), which usually took place shortly before a large-scale attack, were the first reliable indication of an imminent Russian offensive. MS # T-10 describes how those offensives were executed.

IV. The Use of Armor

163. The Russian armored force played only a subordinate role at the beginning of the war. In the advance of 1941, most German troops encountered only smaller units which supported the infantry in the same manner as our self-propelled assault guns. The Russian tanks operated in a very clumsy manner and were quickly eliminated by German

MS # T-22   -87-

antitank weapons. The Russians carried out counterattacks with large tank forces, either alone or in combined operations with other arms, only at individual, important sectors. The intermediate and lower command was still inexperienced, so that the troops usually met with defeat in spite of their valor. Tank losses were often so high that replacements arrived directly from the factories--with mechanics or inadequately trained soldiers as drivers--and were dispatched into combat right off the railway cars.

Ex. 16   The Tank Battle at Raseiniai (June 1941)

App. 7
164. On 23 June 1941 Hoeppner's Panzer Group 4, after a thrust from the area on both sides of Tilsit (East Prussia), had reached the Dubysa, and there had formed several bridgeheads. The 6th Panzer Division, an element of this group, succeeded after bitter fighting in breaking through the elevated enemy positions on both sides of Raseiniai and in taking the city. A follow-up thrust reached the Dubysa, and two bridgeheads were formed. The defeated enemy infantry units scattered into the extensive forests and high grain fields, and constituted a threat to our supply lines.

165. As early as 25 June the Russians launched a surprise counterattack on the southern bridgehead with their hastily brought-up XIV Tank Corps, in order to recapture Raseiniai. They overpowered the 6th Motorcycle Battalion which was committed in the bridgehead, took the bridge, and pushed on in the direction of the city. The 114th Armored Infantry Regiment, reinforced by two artillery battalions and one hundred tanks, was immediately put into action and stopped the main body of the enemy forces. Then there suddenly appeared for the first time a battalion of heavy enemy tanks of previously unknown type. They overran the armored infantry regiment and broke through into the artillery position. The projectiles of all defense weapons (except the 88-mm. Flak) bounced off the thick enemy armor. Our hundred tanks were unable to check the twenty enemy dreadnaughts, and suffered

losses. Several Czech-built tanks (T 36's) that had bogged down in the grain fields because of mechanical trouble were flattened by the enemy monsters. The same fate befell a 150-mm. medium howitzer battery, which kept on firing until the last minute. Despite the fact that it scored direct hit after direct hit from as close a range as two hundred meters, its heavy shells were unable to put even a single tank out of action. The situation became critical. Only the 88-mm. Flak finally knocked out a few of the Russian KV I's and forced the others to withdraw into the woods.

166. One of those heavy tanks even managed to reach the only supply route of the task force (Kampfgruppe) located in the northern bridgehead, and blocked it for several days. The first unsuspecting trucks to arrive with supplies were immediately shot afire by the tank. There were practically no means of eliminating the monster. It was impossible to by-pass the tank because of the swampy surrounding terrain. Neither supplies nor ammunition were brought up. The severely wounded could not be removed to the hospital for the necessary operations, and so they died. The attempt to put the tank out of action with the 50-mm. antitank gun battery, which had just been introduced at that time, at a range of five hundred meters ended with heavy losses to crews and equipment of the battery. The tank, however, remained undamaged in spite of the fact that, as was later determined, we scored fourteen direct hits. They merely produced blue spots on its armor. When a camouflaged 88 was brought up, the tank calmly permitted it to be put into position at a distance of seven hundred meters, and then smashed it and its crew before it was even ready to fire. The attempt of engineers to blow it up at night likewise proved abortive. To be sure, the engineers managed to get to the tank after midnight, and laid the prescribed demolition charge under the caterpillar tracks. The charge went off according to plan, but was insufficient for the oversized tracks. Pieces were broken off the tracks, but the tank remained mobile and continued to molest the rear of the front and to block all supplies. At first it received supplies at night from scattered enemy groups and civilians, but we later prevented this procedure by blocking off the surrounding area. However, even this isolation did not induce it to give up its favorable position. It finally became the victim of a German

ruse. Fifty tanks were ordered to feign an attack from three sides and to fire on it so as to draw all of its attention in those directions. Under the protection of this feint it was possible to set up and camouflage another 88-mm. Flak to the rear of the tank, so that this time it actually was able to fire. Of the twelve direct hits scored by this medium gun, three pierced the tank and destroyed it.

167. The enemy had not taken advantage of the critical situation of the Division which had resulted from the employment of the heavy, 65-ton tanks (Ed: Apparently 65 metric tons, or 71.5 short tons.). His infantry, which had broken through, did not become active again, but passively watched the proceedings. Therefore, it was possible to withdraw strong forces from the northern bridgehead and send them against the rear of the attacking Tank Corps. The latter immediately abandoned its success and retired to the east bank of the river. There, despite the fact that strong neighboring armored forces had already enveloped it and were attacking from the rear, it again held out far too long. The result was that the enemy tank corps lost the bulk of its tanks in the swamps. The infantry scattered and made its way through the woods along swamp paths.

Ex. 17

168. On 26 June 1941 the Russians, by a tank corps thrust, wanted to relieve their forces which were encircled near Rawa Ruska, north of Lwow. This tank corps consisted only of tank chassis mounting machine guns and guns up to 150 mm.; it had no motorized infantry support. Near Magierow it encountered the organized defense of the 97th Light Infantry Division in a day and night attack, and was repulsed. Sixty-three Russian armored vehicles were knocked out.

Ex. 18

The Thrust on Vyazma (Early October 1941)

App. 8

169. In the thrust on Vyazma the 6th Panzer Division, committed in the main effort, reached the upper Dnepr on 4 October 1941, and captured the two bridges there by a coup de main. That maneuver cut off enemy forces which were still west of the river, and assured a continued thrust to the east.

170. On the following day the enemy attempted to parry this severe blow by means of a flank attack. One hundred tanks drove against the road hub of Kholm from the south. They were, for the most part, medium tanks, against which we could send only forty light tanks and one armored infantry company. However, these weak forces were sufficient to contain the dangerous thrust until antiaircraft and antitank guns could be organized into an adequate antitank defense between Kholm and the southern Dnepr bridge. Split up by our tanks in forest fighting, the enemy never succeeded in making a powerful, unified tank thrust. His leading elements were knocked out as they encountered our antitank front. As a result, he became even more timid and scattered his forces in breadth and depth in such a way that all his subsequent tank thrusts, carried out in detail by small groups, could be met by the antitank front and smashed. Kholm and the Dnepr bridge, as well as their connecting road--which the enemy had already taken under intermittent tank fire--remained in our hands. After eighty enemy tanks had been put out of action, a break was made through the strongly fortified position on the east bank of the Dnepr, which was occupied by enemy reserves, and the thrust from the southern bridgehead continued without concern for the enemy.

The flank attack in detail of the hundred enemy tanks near Kholm succeeded in delaying, but not in stopping, the advance of the 6th Panzer Division.

171. While the division with all its combat elements was now rolling along a road deep into enemy territory, hastily assembled Russian tank units and infantry, supported by several batteries, attempted to attack the 40-kilometer flank of the march column and to stop its advance. Some of the Soviet batteries remained in their former positions and merely turned their guns around, while others rushed up at full speed and assumed fire positions in the open. Enemy infantry and tanks advanced in a widespread chain against the German column, and the artillery immediately opened fire with every battery as soon as it had shifted its front.

172. The attack turned out badly for the enemy. In an instant the Division was firing all its weapons at him. The Division resembled a mighty battleship,

MS # T-22   -91-

smashing all targets within reach with the heavy caliber of its broadsides. Artillery and mortar shells from 300 throats of fire hailed down on the enemy batteries and tanks. Soon the enemy tanks were in flames, the enemy batteries transformed into smoking heaps of rubble, and the lines of skirmishers swept away by a swath of fire from hundreds of machine guns. In twenty minutes the work of destruction was completed. The advance continued and on the same day reached Vyazma, its objective. This completed the encirclement of 400,000 Russians.

173. The enemy clearly recognized and twice tried to prevent the Division's intent to break out of the bridgehead and push eastward from Kholm. He failed each time, although he had adequate forces and means at his disposal. In both cases the Russian command was at fault. In the first instance it was unable to execute a co-ordinated blow with a force of a hundred tanks; in the second instance it did not succeed in readying and co-ordinating all the available forces and antitank defenses in time.

174. The command of large tank units was usually difficult for the Russians even in later years. They had only a handful of good armored commanders. In the tank force, too, successes were achieved only by the reckless use of masses. However, those tactics failed whenever even relatively adequate defense means were available on the German side.

Ex. 19   175. In the winter of 1942-43 the Russians employed four tank corps to make a break-through near Kamenka on the Donets. By a thrust on Voroshilovgrad, the Russians would have been able to strike a crushing strategic blow at the deep left flank of Army Group von Manstein on the south bank of the Donets. Instead, they were attracted by Kamenka and Millerovo. Thus, they made an assault only against the wings of a provisional army (Armeeabteilung) which were strongly defended at that point, and in spite of their superiority achieved only a tactical success. At that time the attack of the Russian main force came as a surprise. In minor thrusts launched during the preceding days the Russians had probed the front of this "army", which consisted only of separate strong points (a frontage of two hundred kilometers, held by one infantry division, one reinforced mountain infantry regiment, one SS regiment reinforced by armor, one panzer battalion, and several Flak batteries). The Russians proved that they were still unable at that time to employ large tank units strategically.

The Tank Battle at Kharkov (August 1943)

Ex. 20
App. 9

176. During the course of the well-commanded Russian counteroffensive of Byelgorod (5 August 1943), massed enemy tanks reached the area around Bogodukhov, northwest of Kharkov, and Graivoron on the first day, and then flowed out like lava into the broad plain east of the Vorskla, where they were halted by German counteroperations from the Poltava--Akhtirka area.

177. Kharkov constituted a deep German salient to the east, which prevented the enemy from making use of this important traffic and supply center. All previous Russian attempts to take Kharkov had failed. Neither tank assaults nor infantry mass attacks had succeeded in bringing about the fall of this large city. Reports made by the Russian radio, and by our own pilots, announcing the entry of Russian troops into Kharkov at a time when the German front stood unwavering, did not alter the facts. When the Russian command perceived their mistake, but did not wish to broadcast to the whole world that it was merely thousands of <u>Russian prisoners</u> who had marched into the city, <u>Marshal Stalin</u> ordered the immediate capture of Kharkov.

178. The rehabilitated Russian Fifth Tank Army was assigned this mission. The XI Infantry Corps, however, whose five divisions firmly sealed off the city in a long arc, recognized the new danger in time. It was clear that the Russian Fifth Tank Army would not make a frontal assault on the projecting Kharkov bastion, but would attempt to break through the narrowest part of the arc west of the city, the so-called bottleneck, in order to encircle Kharkov. Antitank defenses were installed at once. All available antitank guns were set up on the northern edge of the bottleneck, which rose like a bastion, and numerous 88-mm. Flak guns were set up in the depth of the bastion. These means would not have been sufficient to repulse the expected mass attack of enemy tanks, but at the last moment the requested 2d SS Panzer Division ("Das Reich") arrived with strong armored forces and was immediately dispatched to the sector most endangered.

179. The 96 Panthers, 32 Tigers, and 25 self-propelled assault guns had hardly taken their assigned positions when the first large-scale attack of the Russian Fifth Tank Army got under way. The first hard German blow, however, hit the assembled masses of enemy tanks which had been recognized while they were still assembling in the villages and the flood plains of a brook valley. Escorted by German fighters, which cleared the sky of Russian aircraft within a few minutes, wings of heavily laden Stukas came on in wedge formation and unloaded their cargoes of destruction in well-aimed dives on the assembled tanks. Dark fountains of earth erupted skyward, and were followed by heavy thunderclaps and shocks which resembled an earthquake. These were the heaviest, 2,000-kilogram bombs, designed for use against enemy battleships, which were all the Luftwaffe had to counter the enemy attack. Wing after wing approached with majestic calm, and carried out its work of destruction without interference. Soon all of the villages occupied by enemy tanks were in flames. A sea of dust and smoke clouds illuminated by the setting sun hung over the brook valley. Dark mushrooms of smoke from burning tanks, victims of the heavy air attacks, stood out in sharp contrast. This gruesome picture bore witness to an undertaking that left death and destruction in its wake. It had hit the enemy so hard that he could no longer launch the projected attack on that day, in spite of Stalin's order. A severe blow had been inflicted on the enemy, and the time needed for organizing our own measures had been gained.

180. The next day the enemy avoided mass grouping of tanks, crossed the brook valley at several places, and disappeared into the broad cornfields which were located ahead of the front but ended at the east-west main highway several hundred meters in front of the main line of resistance. During the night, enemy motorized infantry had already infiltrated through the thin defense lines in several places, and made a surprise penetration near Lyubotin into the artillery position. After stubborn fighting with the gun crews, twelve howitzers without breechblocks—which the crews took with them—fell into enemy hands. The points of the infiltrated motorized infantry already were shooting it out with our local security in the wood adjoining the corps command post.

181. During the morning enemy tanks had worked their way

forward in the hollows up to the southern edges of the cornfields. Now they made a mass dash across the road in full sight. The leading waves of Russian T 34's were caught in the fierce defensive fire of the 96 Panthers, and were on fire before they could reach the main line of resistance. But wave after wave followed, until they flowed across in the protecting hollows and pushed forward into the battle position. Here they were trapped in the net of antitank and antiaircraft guns, Hornets, and Wasps*,

---
*Ed: Hornet (later, Rhinoceros): 88-mm. tank destroyer
Wasp: Self-propelled 105-mm. light field howitzer

---

were split up, and large numbers of them put out of action. The last waves were still attempting to force a break-through in concentrated masses when they were attacked by our Tigers and self-propelled assault guns, which until then had remained as mobile reserves behind the front, and were repulsed with heavy losses.

The first thrust of the enemy was repelled. The price he paid for this mass tank assault amounted to 184 knocked-out T 34's.

182. In the meantime, infantry reserves supported by self-propelled assault guns from the 3d Panzer Division had captured the lost battery positions together with all pieces, and, west of Lyubotin, behind our main line of resistance, had bottled up the battalion or so of infiltrated enemy motorized infantry. Stubbornly defending themselves, the Russians awaited the help that their radio had promised.

183. The enemy changed his tactics, and the next day attacked farther east in a <u>single deep wedge</u>, using several hundred tanks simultaneously. But even while they moved across open terrain along the railroad, numerous tanks were set on fire at a range of two kilometers by the long-range weapons of the Tigers and Hornets. The large-scale enemy attack was not launched until late in the forenoon. As the tanks emerged from the cornfields this time, they were assailed by the concentrated defense of all Tigers, Hornets, Panthers, self-propelled assault guns, and antiaircraft and antitank guns, and the attack collapsed in a short time with the loss of 154 tanks. The weak rifle units which followed were mowed down by the concentrated fire of infantry and artillery as they emerged from the corn-

fields. The encircled motorized battalion had waited in vain for aid, but continued to fight on with incredible tenacity. In the late afternoon its radio announced the defeat of the unit and then fell silent forever. After 48 hours of heroic defense the battalion was killed to the last man, including radio operators.

184. The losses thus far incurred by the enemy were enormous. However, he still possessed more than a hundred tanks, and experience had taught that further attacks were to be expected, even though they were predestined to failure in view of the now vastly superior defense. The few tank crew members taken prisoner were aware that death, or, if they were lucky, capture, awaited every one of their comrades.

185. Contrary to all expectations, an eerie calm prevailed throughout the following day. Several enemy tanks crawled about in the cornfields and towed the damaged tanks away in order to reinforce their greatly depleted ranks. Summer heat simmered over the bloody fields of the past days of battle. A last glow of sunset brought the peaceful day to a close. Might the enemy have given up his plan, or even refused to obey the supreme order to commit hara-kiri with all his forces, to which a repetition of the attack amounted? No, never! He would come back even if he had to pay for it with the last man and the last tank: that was clear to everyone.

186. He did come back, and on the same day. Before midnight, considerable noise from tanks in the cornfields betrayed his approach. The Russian intended to achieve during the night what he had failed to gain by daylight attacks.

187. Before he had reached the foot of the elevated terrain, numerous flashes from firing tanks had ripped the pitch-black darkness of the night and illuminated a mass attack of the entire Russian Tank Army on a broad front. Tanks knocked out at close range already were burning like torches, and lighting up portions of the battlefield. More tanks joined them. The antitank guns could no longer fire properly, since they could hardly distinguish between friend and foe; our own tanks had entered the fray of battle, ramming enemy tanks in a counterthrust or piercing them with shells at gun-barrel range in order to block the break-through. A steady increase in the flash and thunder of tank,

antitank, and antiaircraft guns could be perceived after midnight. The main force of our own tanks had launched a counterattack. Many tanks and several farm buildings went up in flames. The plateau on which this great night tank duel was fought was illuminated by their pale light. This made it possible to recognize the contours of enemy tanks at a distance of more than one hundred meters, and to shell them. The thunderous roll turned into a din like the crescendo of kettledrums as the two main tank forces clashed. Gun flashes from all around ripped the darkness of night throughout an extensive area. For kilometers, armor-piercing projectiles whizzed in all directions into the night. Gradually the pandemonium of the tank battle shifted to the north. However, flashes also appeared farther and farther behind our own front, and fiery torches stood out against the night sky. Not until two or three hours later was calm restored in the depth of our front. The conflict also gradually subsided in the battle position.

188. First reports on the course of the night tank battle were contradictory and gave a confused picture. The situation could be clarified only after daybreak. The most important result established was that the battle was won. There were still enemy tanks and motorized infantry in and behind our own position. Here and there a small gap still remained to be closed. The mopping up of the battle position, however, lasted all morning. By noon the entire position was in our hands and again ready for defense. Only a small patch of woodland, close behind our main line of resistance, was still occupied by enemy motorized infantry supported by a few tanks and antitank guns. All attempts to retake this patch of woods had failed with heavy German losses. Even heavy, concerted fires of strong artillery units could not force the enemy to yield. The tenacious resistance of the enemy was ended only by an attack of flame-throwing tanks, which burned the entire strip of woods to the ground. The foremost of the enemy tanks which had made the deep forward thrust was captured at the western outskirts of Kharkov by one of our divisional headquarters, and the crew members were taken prisoner. All the rest were put out of action by Flak teams.

189. Thus, the enemy's plan to take Kharkov by a large-

scale night attack of the entire Tank Army had failed. More than eighty burned-out tanks, many hundreds of dead, thousands of wounded, and a considerable amount of captured equipment were the outcome of this night battle. It was also the end of the Russian Fifth Tank Army. This army, in the reckless employment of its resources in the effort to recapture Kharkov, lost 420 tanks in three days of fighting, and suffered such heavy losses of men and equipment that it ceased to be a combat factor for the foreseeable future. Kharkov, on the other hand, continued to remain in German hands until the higher command, in consideration of the over-all situation, ordered the retirement of the troops stationed there.

190. Blunders on the part of the leaders were only partially responsible for the fact that every one of these enemy tank attacks failed, although the troops fought with extraordinary bravery. On the other hand, it was striking that the enemy had only weak infantry and artillery forces, and that his air forces did not participate effectively enough in operations. For these reasons the tank forces could not be adequately supported and their successes could not be exploited. The Fifth Tank Army seems to have been forced to premature action for reasons of prestige by binding orders of the Russian Supreme Command.

191. Whether executed by friend or foe, attacks inspired by such motives, in which tactical necessities generally were overlooked, have always exacted heavy casualties and resulted in failure.

Ex. 21   The Break-Through in the Dnepr Bend south of Dnepropetrovsk (1943-44)

192. In the winter of 1943-44, the XXX Infantry Corps' 16th Panzer Grenadier Division experienced a breakthrough of strong Russian tank forces with a long-range objective in the Dnepr bend south of Dnepropetrovsk. Here the Russians, with tank divisions followed by motorized forces, made a deep thrust against the left flank of the German Sixth Army forces which were withdrawing in front of Nikopol.* As this strong tank thrust gained in

----
*Ed: At that time, the German front enclosed Nikopol in a semicircle east of the city.
----

depth, it decreased in power because it split up. It did not achieve its strategic objective. In spite of the fact that the enemy was many times superior in numbers, the Sixth Army succeeded in containing the thrust in the depth of its sector and in forming new fronts. Even after a double envelopment by far superior tank forces (nine tank corps), the Russians, after having encircled the Sixth Army in Bessarabia, did not succeed in blocking the road over the Transylvanian Alps to the remnants of the Sixth and Eighth Armies. In the tank battle of Debrecen (summer 1944), too, Russian tanks and motorized units split up in such a manner, without being reconcentrated, that the weak German panzer divisions, mere skeletons, succeeded not only in preventing a break-through but also in throwing the enemy far back again toward Debrecen. The leadership of these large, strategic armored forces was inadequate. In this instance, too, only the enemy's enormous numerical superiority, and his mobility, brought him local successes.

193. Even in the last months of the war the Russians committed serious blunders in the command of their armored forces. They still failed to understand how to exploit their successes fully. They continued either to advance timidly when there was scarcely any resistance left, or else they carried out deep, isolated tank thrusts, which the infantry was unable to follow and which, consequently, could not lead to permanent success. Russian armored forces always incurred severe losses wherever they encountered German armor still organized in units of any appreciable strength. Thus, as late as April 1945, the battle-weary 6th Panzer Division succeeded, in what was probably the last tank battle, in repulsing vastly superior Russian tank forces in the plains of the lower March River, and in knocking out eighty tanks.

194. If the Russian tank forces with their vastly superior numbers had had proper leadership, the Russians would have been able to

bring about the end of the war at a much earlier stage.

Chapter Four
DEFENSE

I. General

195. There are two conspicuous characteristics of the Russian soldier, both of which are inherent in the Russian people, and both of which were in evidence during the course of the two World Wars: stubbornness and tenacity in the defense, inflexibility and little adaptability in the attack.

196. During World War I the power of resistance of the Russian soldier gradually became paralyzed by a lack of heavy weapons, the great inferiority of Russian artillery, the almost complete lack of aircraft, and by the fact that the morale of the Russian Army was undermined more and more as time went on. As early as 1915 Russian units left their trenches at the onset of German attacks, came toward the attackers, and surrendered. Such incidents, however, were not characteristic of the Russian soldier, but rather an indication of conditions prevailing at that time. Elite units, such as the Guards, and ably commanded troops defended themselves with extreme tenacity even in World War I.

197. In World War II, particularly during its first phase, there also were numerous examples of Russian soldiers showing but little power of resistance, throwing away their rifles, and surrendering or deserting by the thousands. This, however, occurred only in

great battles of encirclement where the Russian soldier became demoralized by the impossibility of continuing the battle successfully, or by Stuka attacks and heavy, concentrated artillery fire. In general, in this war, strict leadership, good equipment, emphasis on patriotism, and the fear--stimulated by propaganda--of falling into enemy hands, resulted in a tenacity of defense which made attacks without tanks, despite artillery and air support, extremely costly or even futile. This power of resistance on the part of the Russian soldier increased during the course of the war in a direct ratio to the decrease of the German power of attack, because the numerical superiority of the Russians became more and more crushing, their equipment continued to improve as compared with German equipment, and continuous military successes lifted their spirit and their confidence.

198. The speed with which the Russian disappears into the earth is typical. A system of field fortifications with numerous earthworks of all kinds is constructed within the shortest imaginable time. The laying of a large number of mines of various types and the stringing of barbed wire also take very little time. The troops are deployed in depth; they frequently change the strength of forces occupying a position (even to the extent of varying the strength of the day and night shifts), and a careful plan of fire for all weapons is immediately organized. Except during great battles, there is but little firing activity, chiefly maintained by the infantry heavy weapons, particularly mortars (80-mm. and 120-mm.), which are employed flexibly and in great numbers. In raids, and even in attacks against

Russian positions, it was usually quite a while before effective defense fire of the Russian artillery began. But even after such a long interval the Russian artillery was unable to direct its fire precisely and flexibly. The emphasis of the defense was on the infantry weapons, including antitank and self-propelled assault guns, and on extensive mine laying.

199. The defensive power of the Russian troops is none too good, if the attacker builds up a strong superiority in air and ground weapons, and provides for sufficient depth of the attacking force. Above all, the attacker must <u>start determinedly</u> and must know how to exploit each success <u>quickly and flexibly</u> in order to achieve freedom of movement as rapidly as possible. If an energetic command, planning on a large scale, knows how to make use of the <u>initiative</u> which it seizes, it will certainly be successful, because the Russian command does not possess the necessary speed of action in unexpected situations.

200. The Russian was a master of the defense. He attained excellent results not only in construction of positions, but also in camouflage, and in the construction of dummy installations. By unscrupulous use especially of the civilian population (including women and children), he created well-developed zones in depth. In open terrain he dug wide and deep antitank ditches, many kilometers long, forward of his front. Mine fields, wire obstacles, entanglements, and other obstacles were immediately set up everywhere. If, because of the nature of terrain, he expected tank attacks, he developed points of main effort. He was very adept at using villages as strong points. Wherever he could,

he set up flanking weapons. As far as the infantry was concerned, he conducted his defense in a mobile manner, but within his defense trenches. He made considerable use of roving guns. He accomplished surprise fires mostly with heavy mortars and numerous multibarreled rocket projectors (Stalinorgeln). He made little use of methodical artillery harassing fire. Upon the loss of parts of a position, reserves for a counterthrust were always quickly at hand. Counterthrusts and counterattacks were in most instances supported by tanks. He did not often conduct counterattacks that were based on a preconceived plan, since, from the standpoint of leadership, they were too difficult for him. From 1943 on, he strengthened his defense by mass employment of antiaircraft guns and flame throwers in so-called antitank-gun fronts, which were superbly camouflaged and dangerous for tank attacks. Daytime observation was made difficult, because he showed almost no movement. In general, one might say that the Russian undertook his defense in open terrain as well as in wooded areas according to principles rigidly drilled into the soldiers, and that he showed little imagination in developing new methods of battle. He relied, in attack as well as in defense, on reckless employment of manpower.

201. Another peculiarity to be mentioned is the fact that the Russian proved himself to be very well disciplined in opening fire. He waited calmly until the enemy had approached to a favorable range, and then he opened surprise fire. Our combat reconnaissance always had to be on the lookout in order to avoid unnecessary losses. The Russian

sniper battalions particularly excelled in fire discipline.

202. In 1941 the Russian also supported his defense action in the Parpach position in the Crimea very adroitly and effectively from the sea by artillery flanking fire.

II. Use of Mines

203. The Russian made extensive use of mines. As a rule, a protective mine belt was to be found about eight to ten meters in front of the most forward trench. Terrain particularly favorable for an enemy approach likewise was heavily mined. The Russian preferred to employ wooden box mines, which could not be detected by the standard mine detectors. In the depth of the battle position, mines were laid in unexpected places. In favorable terrain, antitank mines were very numerous.

204. Difficulties in the transport of Teller mines due to lack of transport space were, according to PW information, solved in a very primitive manner. When marching up to the front as relief, every man had to carry two antitank mines. At the front, these mines were laid by the engineers according to a diagrammed mine plan.

205. In 1944-45 the Russians, while on the move, also scattered mines around points of main effort in order to block tank attacks. In the Southern Ukraine we saw how the Russians, following a successful tank thrust, immediately protected the terrain they had gained with a belt of antitank mines blocking all roads and approaches. On one day alone, twenty thousand such mines were laid. Our counter-

attacks ground to a halt and collapsed in mine fields of that type.

206. The Russian cleared mines in front of our obstacles during the night, and used them for his own purposes. Later on, we laid mine fields only behind our own front, at points at which a tank break-through or an enemy offensive was to be expected.

207. When the enemy intended to give up a previously defended zone, he used many tricks. He would, for example, attach demolition charges with push-pull igniters to abandoned field kitchens, weapons, corpses, tombstones, etc.; he connected explosive charges to doors, windows, or stoves in the winter; he installed pressure mines under stairs and floors, and booby-trapped abandoned trucks and other equipment.

208. When we took Kiev and Vyborg in 1941, and Sevastopol in 1942, the Russian used <u>remote (radio) controlled</u> mines for blowing up entire blocks of houses as soon as the enemy entered them. This type of remote-controlled ignition was the best solution to the problem ever to come to our attention. The ignition apparatus consisted of three parts, each of which was not much larger than a full brief case. It was easy to move, could easily be built into a hidden spot, and was at first hard to find. Built-in safety devices prevented an accidental or untimely detonation. The ignition apparatus included a clock, which ran only on a certain signal for a certain length of time, and permitted detonation only during certain minutes. There was, furthermore, a code which, when given at a certain speed, was the sole means for setting off the mines.* The ticking of the clocks, however,

---

*Ed: The meaning of the sentence which follows in the German original is not entirely clear. Since it may be presumed that part of the original text has inadvertently been omitted either by the author or the person typing the original text, the entire statement has been omitted from the English version for the sake of clarity. The German original reads as follows: "This fact rendered clearing operations by means of pull- and pressure-release igniters very difficult." (Ein Aufraeumen durch Zug- und Entlastungszuendern [sic] war hiedurch sehr erschwert.)

---

could be heard with sensitive sound detectors and led to the discovery of the ignition apparatus.

209. During the autumn offensive in 1941 against Moscow, the Russian employed so-called mine dogs for destroying German tanks. In the manner of pack animals, medium-sized dogs carried demolition charges on both sides of their backs. These charges were connected to a spindle fastened to the dog's back. The spindle contained the igniter contact. The dogs were trained to hide under approaching tanks. In so doing, the dog inadvertently brought the upright spindle, which was about 15 centimeters long, into contact with the belly of the tank and set off the charge.

210. News of this insidious improvisation caused some alarm in the panzer units and made them fire at all approaching dogs on sight. The author, who saw action before Moscow with his panzer division, has no knowledge of any case where a German tank was destroyed by a Russian mine dog. On the other hand, Russian prisoners of war reported that several mine dogs fleeing from the fire of German tanks sought protection underneath Russian tanks, which promptly blew up. One thing is

certain: the specter of the mine dogs ceased just as abruptly as it had begun.

III. Conduct of Battle

211. The Russian defended every inch of his soil with incredible tenacity. At the beginning of the war he was conversant only with long defense lines, which he strengthened by employing an amazing number of personnel for digging trenches. Artillery confined its activities to minor fire concentrations. However, it proved to be more mobile than the infantry, and employed many roving guns which sometimes became very annoying, since they fired only a short time from one position and then reappeared elsewhere. The Russian required a long period of time to bring effective fire to bear against an attack already in progress.

212. In 1943, new methods of tank and antitank warfare were introduced, while the methods of the infantry remained the same. Heavy machine guns and dug-in tanks frequently were encountered deep in the battle position. The latter were particularly dangerous because they were well armored and difficult to hit. In sectors in which the terrain was passable for tanks, antitank-gun fronts would be set up in nearly all instances. They were developed to extraordinary strength and foiled many a German armored attack. They were also used against infantry, in which case they fired high-explosive shells.

213. Although almost all inhabited places were crammed

with troops, they seemed deserted to reconnaissance, since even water and food details were allowed to leave their shelters only after dark.

214. In most cases, tank counterattacks without infantry support were certain to fall victim to German antitank defense. Infantry counterattacks were infrequent and generally too late. For the rest, no important changes took place in Russian defense methods up to the end of the war. The multibarrelled rocket projectors, which the Russians employed more and more, certainly were very effective from a psychological standpoint, but their physical effect was much less impressive. The most dangerous weapons continued to the medium and heavy mortars, particularly after the heavy mortars were concentrated in battalions in 1944.

215. Areas of great importance were surrounded with heavy fortifications. For instance, the German armored units before Leningrad encountered fortification systems up to ten kilometers in depth, including innumerable earth and concrete bunkers with built-in guns and other heavy weapons. There were even concrete pillboxes with disappearing armored cupolas for artillery and machine guns. They were constructed in the rear area from standard concrete forms, assembled at the front, and equipped with the armored cupolas. The raising and lowering of the cupolas was accomplished by means of improvised wooden levers, which had to be operated manually by the pillbox crew. A speedy elimination of these concrete pillboxes with the means available in mobile warfare was difficult.

216. The forward edge of such a defense system was generally

situated behind an antitank ditch many kilometers long and up to six meters wide and four meters deep. Embedded in the rear wall of this ditch were dugouts housing the riflemen with their defense weapons. A second and third antitank ditch frequently would be located in the depth of the system, and connected by a cross ditch so as to prevent enemy tanks that had penetrated the position from rolling it up. A machine-gun or antitank bunker in every bend of the antitank ditch afforded flank protection. It was not unusual to encounter dammed-up watercourses close to the fortified position. They were up to a hundred meters wide and several meters deep, and presented an obstacle difficult to overcome. The Russians eliminated all favorable approaches to their front (forests, underbrush, tall grain fields, etc.) by laying extensive mine fields.

217. Outposts were located ahead of the fortified position wherever possible. Such outposts always had engineers attached whose mission it was to block routes of approach with a substantial number of mines or other obstacles.

Ex. 22

App. 10

The Russian Defensive Effort during the German Break-Through of the Leningrad Line in the Fortified Krasnogvardeysk Region (September 1941)

218. The area of Krasnogvardeysk, south of Leningrad, had been developed according to the above-mentioned principles into an outlying fortress. During early September 1941, it presented great difficulties to the advance of several German corps. Krasnogvardeysk blocked all highways and railroads leading to Leningrad from the south, thus constituting a main bulwark of Russian resistance. The Russians defended it tenaciously. Repeated attacks by several infantry divisions were repulsed. Only in the course

of a general attack on the Leningrad Line, and after bitter pillbox fighting in the area immediately surrounding Krasnogvardeysk, was that town finally taken from the rear by a carefully prepared surprise break-through to the west of it. This typical example of the Russian method of defending a methodically fortified zone, and its capture by means of an adroitly led attack, will be discussed in detail in the following paragraphs.

219. Appendix 10 shows the defense system of Krasnogvardeysk. That system had been prepared long in advance, and consisted of an outer belt of concrete and earth bunkers, with numerous intermediate installations which were interconnected by trench systems that could easily be defended. There were tank-proof watercourses or swamps almost everywhere in front of the outer defense belt. Where this natural protection was lacking, wide antitank ditches had been dug.

220. From one to three kilometers behind the outer defense belt was an inner one consisting of a heavily fortified position encircling the periphery of the town. Just north of the town ran the continuous Leningrad Line, with which the defense system of Krasnogvardeysk was integrated. It constituted, simultaneously, the rear protection of the town and the covering position in case the town should have to be evacuated. Beyond the open, elevated terrain immediately west of Krasnogvardeysk lay an extensive forest zone. Within that zone, a few hundred meters from its eastern edge, ran the western front of the outer defense belt. At that point it consisted of wood and earth bunkers, trenches, and strong points--all approaches to which were barricaded by extensive mine fields, abatis, and multiple rows of barbed wire. Located from three to four kilometers farther west were mobile security detachments. Attached to these were engineer units for the laying of scattered mines.

221. The cornerstone of this position was the heavily fortified and mined village of Salyzy, located at the southern end of the forest zone. It covered a road leading to Krasnogvardeysk from the west, and another one which branched off the former to the north within Salyzy. The latter road served as supply route for all the troops situated west of it in the forest position. It crossed the dammed-up Ishora River via a bridge located in front of the

Leningrad Line, traversing it in a northwesterly direction. At that point the Line consisted of four trench systems, one behind the other, with numerous machine-gun, antitank-gun, and artillery bunkers.

222. The 6th Panzer Division, advancing on Krasnogvardeysk from the west via Salyzy, had the mission of breaking through the Leningrad Line in the above-described area, and attacking Krasnogvradeysk from the rear. Following a plan of attack based on precise aerial photos, the Division decided to push with concentrated force through the outer defense belt at Salyzy, to follow through with a northward thrust and break through the Leningrad Line, and then to roll up the latter to the east. The main body of the Division attacked on the road and along the edge of the forest running parallel to it, took the antitank ditch after a brief engagement, and, during the noon hours, also captured the village of Salyzy after having stormed a large number of bunkers. A bunker at the edge of the forest continued to offer resistance until late afternoon.

223. Immediately after breaking into the village, the armored elements of the Division, supported by an artillery battalion, advanced through the rear of the enemy-occupied forest position against the Leningrad Line. Under cover of tank fire, the engineers took the undamaged bridge in a coup de main and removed prepared demolition charges. About six kilometers north of Salyzy, panzer grenadiers (armored infantry) following them penetrated the antitank ditch, which began at the bridge and ran at a right angle to the front, and formed a bridgehead. During the evening the main body of the Division cleared the surrounding forests of enemy forces and, with a front turned 90 degrees, assembled in them for a northward thrust to join the forces at the bridgehead, which meanwhile had been cut off by the enemy. On the evening of the same day a panzer grenadier battalion succeeded in breaking through the inner defense ring located east of Salyzy behind a river arm, in the area of the neighboring SS Police Division, which had been stalled along its entire front. The bridgehead thus established by the battalion opened a gateway to Krasnogvardeysk for the SS Police Division.

224. On the second day of attack the bulk of the 6th Panzer Division advanced along the road up to the

armored units in the northern bridgehead. Some of its elements mopped up enemy forces on the plateau west of Krasnogvardeysk, while other ones rolled up the enemy forest position which was pinning down a unit that had been detached as a flank guard on the previous day.* During the forenoon the entire

---

*Ed: The German original reads, "...while other ones rolled up the enemy forest position, a unit of which, detached as flank guard on the previous day, was still holding out." (...und rollte mit anderen Kraeften die feindliche Waldstellung auf, von der noch immer ein am Vortag als Seitenhut ausgeschiedener Verband festlag.) The German construction, as well as the general context, point to a typing error in the original, substituting "von" for "vor".

---

attack area south of the Leningrad Line was cleared of the enemy. Along the northern wing of the position on the forest edge alone, forty thousand Russian mines were picked up and disarmed. Then, battalion after battalion was pushed through the bridgehead into the antitank ditch, about 3 kilometers long, which ran up to a forest area. These battalions were pushed so far to the north that the four parallel defense systems of the Leningrad Line could be rolled up simultaneously from the flank by one battalion each. A desperate enemy attempt at repelling the advance of the battalions and tanks by means of a cavalry attack was easily foiled. The antitank ditch, four meters wide and deep, had made it possible to change the attack front of the entire division again by 90 degrees at one fell swoop. Under cover of flank and rear protection, bunker after bunker, and strong point after strong point was now blasted by Stukas, medium artillery, antitank and antiaircraft guns, and captured; step by step the trenches and nests of resistance were cleaned out. All our artillery was still in the old front south of the Leningrad Line, and its fire thus formed a complete flanking curtain in front of the attacking battalions.

225. The railroad running through the attack area was reached on the second day of battle, and the Krasnogvardeysk--Leningrad highway on the third day. There, our forces took a group of artillery pillboxes equipped with disappearing armored cupolas. At that

point the Division stood directly in the rear of the town. The enemy, forced to retreat hurriedly, had only one side road available for a withdrawal, and that road lay under the effective artillery fire of the Panzer Division. With serious losses, the enemy divisions poured back over this road and the adjoining terrain. The attempt of the motorized medium artillery, which was the first of the enemy forces to disengage, at escaping on the wide asphalt road via Pushkin, failed. The road was already blocked by our armor. All the enemy artillery, as well as all the other enemy motor vehicles, were set afire by our armor when they attempted to break through at this point. During the following night the enemy managed to evacuate the town and escape with a black eye. He then re-established himself with strong rear guards on high terrain between Krasnogvardeysk and Pushkin.

226. The next day, pursuing infantry divisions again bogged down before these heavily fortified enemy positions. Here the enemy had employed the most modern system of field fortifications ever encountered on the Eastern Front. All of the fortification installations were <u>underground</u>. The defense was carried out in subterranean passages which were established along terrain steps and were equipped with well-camouflaged embrasures. The heavy weapons likewise were in subterranean emplacements which were invisible from the outside. There were also subterranean rooms quartering ten to twenty men each, ammunition dumps, and medical and supply installations. All installations were interconnected by underground communication passages. The entrances were situated several hundred meters farther to the rear, well camouflaged by shrubbery and groups of trees, and protected by open squad trenches and several standard bunkers which could only be recognized from nearby. Neither the best ground nor air reconnaissance could spot this fortification system even at close range. Not even after its guns had opened fire could it be located, as a result of which it proved very difficult to neutralize. All frontal assaults of the infantry were unsuccessful.

227. Not until two days later was it possible to clarify the situation and to capture the position. By that time the 6th Panzer Division, committed as an encircling force maneuvering via Posyolok Taytsy,

was pivoting into the rear of the Russian fortifications. An odd coincidence played into the hands of the Division. The previous evening strong reconnaissance patrols had advanced into the high terrain. Suddenly encountering the rearmost outlying bunker of the position, the patrols took it by storm without orders. Among the captured garrison was a Russian military engineer, the builder of this fortification system. With him, the plans of all the installations fell into German hands, and it was easy to plan the attack for the next day.

228. However, the attack of the lead-off panzer grenadier regiment had hardly begun when a new difficulty arose. The enemy had recognized the danger to his frontally impregnable position, and launched an attack from Pushkin against the rear of the 6th Panzer Division. A long column of enemy tanks, the end of which could not even be surmised in the dust, rolled against our own rear guard unit. The first of the enemy tanks had already passed a narrow strip between swamps and turned against the defended elevations. At the head of the main body of the enemy, we spotted 54 KV I's (heavy 65-ton tanks). However, except for one 88-mm. Flak battery and the antitank guns of the rear guard panzer grenadier battalion, our Division had at that moment only one panzer battalion with light Czech tanks available for its defense. The heavy Flak guns were already thundering. Flames from tanks that had sustained hits rose straight toward the sky. The vanguard of enemy tanks spread out, but kept moving ahead. Suddenly it was attacked and destroyed from very close range by a hail of fire from the tank destroyer battalion which had just arrived with 27 heavy antitank guns. Fourteen columns of black smoke announced to the main body of the enemy the destruction of his vanguard. Thereupon the main body suddenly stopped and no longer dared to pass the swamp narrow. Rear elements fanned out and disappeared into the adjoining terrain. Heavy tank fighting indicated that our own panzer regiment, which had been summoned by radio, had gone into action. Soon the din increased. The panzer regiments of the neighboring 1st and 8th Panzer Divisions which had also been summoned attacked the flank and rear of the enemy. The Russian realized his precarious situation and felt himself no longer equal to the task. His losses and his retrograde movements bore evidence to that fact. Even the heavy tanks, only four

of which had been reached and destroyed by the heavy Flak guns, turned and retreated. The enemy had avoided a showdown. The threat to the rear of the Panzer Division had thus been eliminated.

229. In the meantime, however, the panzer grenadier attack, supported by a panzer battalion, continued according to plan. In heavy fighting, the bunkers and squad trenches which protected the enemy's rear were taken one by one, and the entrances to the subterranean defense system reached. During the fighting for the first entrance, the crew resisted from an inner compartment with fire and hand grenades. In this action three Russian medical corps women in uniform, who defended the entrance with hand grenades, also were killed. When their bodies were removed, several hand grenades were found on them.

230. The mopping up of the subterranean passages was time-consuming and difficult. It had to be carried out by specially trained shock troops with hand grenades and machine pistols. Our attempts to clear out the strong bunker crews led to bitter underground hand-to-hand fighting with heavy losses on both sides. The enemy defended himself to the utmost. The attack stalled. Only after engineer demolition teams had succeeded in determining the location of the subterranean bunkers by noting the sparser growth of grass above them, could these bunkers be blown up by heavy demolition charges from above, and taken. But the closer the shock troops came to the front position of the enemy's defense system, the more serious became our losses. The engineer demolition teams and all the other units were advancing above the enemy defense system, into the heavy artillery fire supporting the frontally attacking infantry divisions of the neighboring army. Only when roundabout telephone communications had been established, and the devastating fire ordered to cease, was it possible to take the entire subterranean defense system. Now, a junction was effected with our infantry on the other side. Subsequently, our forces also occupied Pushkin.

231. With that, the most tenacious Russian defensive battles of 1941, between Krasnogvardeysk and Leningrad, came to an end. Only the flexible leadership of battle-tested armored forces, attacking with elan, made it possible to overcome the defense zones which

had been set up in an all-out effort of the latest Russian defense technique. Within a week the 6th Panzer Division had had to break through and roll up twelve positions, repel several counterattacks, and take more than three hundred heavily fortified bunkers.

Ex. 23

The Russian Defense System during the Pincers Attack on Kursk (July 1943)

232. Interesting and instructive also was the Russian conduct of battle in the defense against the German pincers attack (Operation ZITADELLE) on Kursk in July 1943.

233. The exhaustion on both sides after the preceding long winter battles led, at this sector of the front, to a pause of three months, which both opponents used to replenish their forces and to prepare for Operation ZITADELLE. The Russian expected the attack precisely at the location and in the manner in which it was undertaken, and prepared his defense accordingly.

234. Behind the most endangered sectors, opposite Byelgorod and Orel, he constructed defense systems of hitherto unknown depth, and strengthened them with all kinds of obstacles. To be prepared against surprise armored thrusts, all points susceptible to enemy penetration were safeguarded up to a depth of fifty kilometers by fully manned antitank-gun fronts, antitank ditches, mine fields, and tanks in emplacements, in such numbers and strength that to overcome them would have called for great sacrifices and much time. Behind the pressure points north of Byelgorod and south of Kursk, sufficient local forces stood ready everywhere. Noteworthy were the numerous alternate firing positions, and the fact that the bulk of the numerous Russian artillery pieces was kept as far to the rear as their maximum range allowed, so as to escape counterbattery fire from German heavy howitzer batteries and to be able, in case of reverses, to support the infantry as long as possible. The enemy batteries preferred firing positions in forests, or in orchards adjacent to inhabited localities. For mobile operations, the Russian very adroitly employed multibarrelled rocket projectors. His strong strategic reserves were assembled farther east, in the region of the Oskol River, in such a manner that after the attacking German divisions had exhausted themselves in the above-mentioned

defense system, the reserves could launch a counter-attack, or, at worst, contain an enemy break-through. In the bulge extending far to the west, however, the Russians had stationed only weak and inferior forces, which were not backed up by any deep defense system. During the long waiting period each side learned all about the enemy situation and intentions down to the last details. The Russians, for instance, broadcast to the German lines by loudspeaker the secret day and hour of attack well in advance, and in the same manner announced two postponements of the offensive. Nevertheless, the German attack was carried out at the precise point at which the enemy expected it. As anticipated, it did not develop into a dynamic offensive, but became a slow wrestling match with an enemy firmly clinging to a maze of trenches and bunkers; an enemy who, unshaken by our preparatory fire, offered dogged resistance. Many positions could only be taken after prolonged hand-grenade duels. The enemy employed stronger tank forces only against what he guessed to be the weakest point in the German attack wedge, i.e., the flank of XI Infantry Corps which attacked on the right wing. Every one of these counter-attacks was repulsed. (See MS # T-21, Example 73.)

235. On the very first day of the attack, 5 July 1943, several German divisions each sustained losses up to 1,000 dead and wounded. The German armor, too, suffered substantial losses each day from the enemy's strong antitank defenses and mine fields. This fact, as well as the divergent directions of thrust of the various corps, visibly diminished the momentum of the attack. When, after about two weeks of bloody fighting, there was no longer any hope of reaching the desired objectives, and when our forces even began to meet reverses in the Orel area, the attack was called off, and previous territorial gains were relinquished. By means of excellent organization of his defenses, and adroit conduct of battle, the enemy had brought about the collapse of the German offensive. Shortly thereafter the enemy launched a counteroffensive with fresh reserves and effected a major break-through.

236. It would certainly have been most awkward for the enemy if the full-strength eleven German panzer divisions and five infantry divisions had not opened the attack, but had waited for him to attack. The possibility of another forward thrust, and the defense against the enemy break-through at Byelgorod are discussed in

MS # T-10.

Ex. 24   The Russian Defense against the German Relief Thrust on Stalingrad (December 1942)

App. 11

237. Conditions were entirely different for the Russians in their defense against the German relief thrust on Stalingrad in December 1942. Here, there existed only temporary field positions, and the defense had to be conducted in a mobile manner. The Russian was not adept at either, a fact which accounts for his failures.

238. Appendix 11 illustrates the grouping for the defense and the direction of the German thrust. At first the Russians pushed a cavalry corps strengthened by armor and camel troops forward along the Don up to the Kurmoyarskiy Aksay River for reconnaissance and for screening the movements of the infantry and tank forces assembling in the rear. The 6th Panzer Division was 10 to 20 percent overstrength and had to conduct the main thrust. When its leading elements arrived, the vanguard of the enemy cavalry corps was just moving into the city [sic] (about 26 November 1942). It was driven back, and the assembly of German forces continued. The attempt to take Kotelnikovo in an assault by the entire cavalry corps on 5 and 6 December 1942, ended in a smashing defeat of the corps at Pokhlebin. Meanwhile, the enemy cautiously advanced two rather weak infantry divisions along both sides of the railroad onto the elevations north of the city, and pushed back several outposts. After the bitter experience of Pokhlebin, however, he did not dare attack Kotelnikovo again. He assembled his main force, the Third Tank Army and additional infantry forces, between the Aksay River and the Mishkova River sector. His entire defense forces were drawn up in three echelons, one behind the other, thirty kilometers in width and seventy kilometers in depth. Our impression was that the enemy would move up under the protection of his advance infantry and cavalry divisions, and then, with his entire tank army, attack the 6th Panzer Division, which was marching up alone, in order to destroy it in the wide forefield of Stalingrad before it reached the city. That enemy move, however, did not materialize. On that occasion the Russians either missed a chance, or else did as yet not feel strong enough for an attack on the Division, which was equipped with two hundred

tanks and self-propelled assault guns, as well as a large number of antitank weapons. Neither did he act to save his reinforced cavalry corps from destruction on 5 and 6 December, and also looked on idly on 12 December while the beginning of the relief thrust of the 6th Panzer Division rolled over his advance infantry divisions and scattered them. The northernmost of the two divisions here lost its entire artillery. The weak remnants of the cavalry corps were also caught on the fringes of the mighty assault and so badly mauled that they played no further part in the course of the offensive.

239. Thus it happened that the 6th Panzer Division, without protection on its northern flank, was able to cross the Aksay River as early as the third day. Its southern wing was protected by the 23d Panzer Division (in regimental strength with fifteen to twenty tanks), which followed in echelons.

240. The crossing of the Aksay River met only weak resistance from advance elements of an enemy mechanized corps, which was soon overcome. In an immediate follow-up thrust by all armored units, Verkhniy-Kumskiy, the keypoint of the assembly area of the Third Russian Tank Army, was taken. Not till then were the enemy tanks stirred to action, but now they displayed very spirited activity. Speed was imperative. Therefore, the enemy was compelled to radio all his orders and reports in the clear. Due to the fact that the Russians were forced to put their cards on the table, our own far inferior forces were able during the ensuing several days of bitter tank fighting to attack enemy elements in lightning moves, and to beat them decisively before they could receive help. In the ensuing melees the enemy occasionally succeeded in concentrating greatly superior forces which threatened to become dangerous to the Division. Our own armored forces then immediately withdrew, only to attack the enemy from the rear again the moment an opportunity presented itself.

241. Both sides made large-scale shifts under cover of darkness. By lightning-like feints and changes of direction, it was repeatedly possible to attack strong enemy tank concentrations simultaneously from all sides in the larger hollows of the hilly terrain, and to destroy them to the last tank. In this manner a

number of so-called tank cemeteries orginated, where from fifty to eighty knocked-out enemy tanks, mostly T 34's, stood in clusters within a small area. Our own bomber wings repeatedly bombed them by mistake. Neither our own, nor enemy aircraft could take any part in the seesaw tank battles, since the opposing tanks were frequently so intermingled that they could not be differentiated. Although air activity on both sides was very lively, it was forced to limit itself to attacking motor pools and supply lines. The air arm was of no decisive importance.

242. While the tank battle north of the Aksay River was still in progress, enemy tank and motorized brigades crossed the river in a southerly direction and attempted to cut off the bridge crossing, which was strongly held on both sides of the river. This had to be avoided under all circumstances, but without depleting the armored forces presently engaged in crucial battles. Soon the bridgehead was surrounded. Although more than a dozen tanks were knocked out, just as many surviving enemy tanks overran the entrenched infantry and penetrated up to a rather large village located in the center of the bridgehead and defended by the 57th Armored Engineer Battalion. Not a single engineer or rifleman deserted his post. Each man became a tank buster. Just as fast as enemy tanks entered the village, they burst into flames, attacked by the elite of the tank busters. Not one escaped. Three times the enemy repeated this assault, and three times he was repulsed. Then a reinforced infantry regiment attacked him from the rear, scattered the entire enemy force, and knocked out fourteen tanks. That opened the route of advance again and assured the free flow of supplies across the bridge.

243. When strong enemy motorized infantry with numerous anti-tank weapons entered the battle at Verkhniy-Kumskiy, and our armored infantry forces were tied down supporting their neighbor and German forces engaged at the Aksay River, our armored units were so severely restricted in their freedom of movement that they had to be pulled back to the Aksay River. The enemy, however, had suffered such heavy tank losses that he did not dare risk the rest of his tanks in a pursuit. He contented himself with defending a long ridge south of Verkhniy-Kumskiy. The premature attempt, ordered by a higher command, to roll up this ridge position from the flank with the

combined armored elements of the 6th and 23d Panzer Divisions failed. Its failure was due to the lack of sufficient infantry for silencing the numerous antitank guns and rifles which were entrenched in deep antitank pits and well camouflaged by high steppe grass. Although it was perfectly possible to roll from one end of the ridge to the other, the enemy motorized riflemen popped up again afterwards like jack-in-the-boxes, and with their numerous antitank rifles knocked out many an armored vehicle. The combined armored force suffered considerable losses and had to be recalled in the evening without having accomplished its mission.

244. Not until two days later did a planned attack of the entire 6th Panzer Division succeed in taking the position and cleaning it out. In the subsequent night attack the armored infantry recaptured the stubbornly defended village of Verkhniy-Kumskiy, destroyed a number of emplaced tanks, numerous antitank guns, and over one hundred antitank rifles. At dawn of the following day the elevated position north of the village was taken in co-operation with the newly arrived 17th Panzer Division, which had only the combat strength of a reinforced battalion. The 11th Panzer Regiment, which up to this time had been held in reserve, was now employed in pursuit, and inflicted heavy losses upon the enemy who was retreating through a single defile.

245. In the midst of the pursuit, however, the Panzer Regiment suddenly had to be halted, and the entire 6th Panzer Division turned 90 degrees to the east in order to rally to the aid of the neighboring 23d Panzer Division on the right, which was being pushed back beyond the Aksay River by a newly arrived rifle corps. The further pursuit toward the north had to be left to the weak 17th Panzer Division, which, however, lacked sufficient driving force to destroy the beaten enemy.

246. The turning of the 6th Panzer Division against the rear of the new enemy had decisively changed the situation of the 23d Panzer Division. The enemy corps immediately broke off its attack and hastily retreated eastward in order to escape the deadly blow that would have been dealt it very soon, had it remained. After all, the enemy tanks and antitank-gun fronts thrown

against the 6th Panzer Division had already been scattered, and our own armor was about to cut off the enemy's escape route. At this critical moment, too, the enemy corps commander radioed his urgent orders in the clear.

247. But the objective of the Panzer Division was Stalingrad, and not the pursuit of a corps in a different direction. Thus, it let the enemy go as soon as the 23d Panzer Division, now relieved of enemy pressure, advanced again. The 6th Panzer Division now turned north and, after hard fighting, reached the Mishkova River sector at Bolshaya Vasilyevka. At that point the Stalingrad garrison was supposed to make contact with the Division. Two bridgeheads were quickly formed, the village taken, and the entire Division concentrated in a small area for mobile defense. It had already covered two-thirds of the distance, and stood 48 kilometers from Stalingrad; the flash of signal rockets from the city could be observed at night. It remains a puzzle why the Sixth Army (Field Marshal Paulus) did not break out at that time (20 December).

248. In forced marches the enemy brought up additional strong forces from the Stalingrad front and the Volga in order to support the beaten Third Tank Army and throw back the German forces. Since he no longer had sufficient tank forces available for this purpose, he hoped to overwhelm and destroy them with the newly formed infantry main-attack army. The brown flood surged forward in multitudes never before encountered. Attack wave followed attack wave without regard for losses. Each one was wiped off the face of the earth by a terrific hail of fire without gaining so much as a foot of ground. Therefore, the masses went around the two flanks of the German Division in order to encircle it. In the course of this maneuver they came between the artillery position and the Panzer Regiment. Firing from all barrels, 150 tanks and self-propelled assault guns attacked the masses from the rear when they tried to escape the hurricane of fire from the artillery. In their desperate situation many Russians threw down their weapons and surrendered. Succeeding elements flowed back; enemy forces which had penetrated into the village were driven out again by a counterthrust of the infantry, and tanks which had broken through were knocked out. The enemy mass assault had col-

lapsed; the once critical situation had been brought under control. The front stood firm as a rock.

249. Thus, on 22 December, the 6th Panzer Division had regained its freedom of movement. By a further forward thrust of thirty kilometers on 24 December, the Division was to help the encircled Sixth Army in breaking out of Stalingrad. That operation, however, never materialized, because the Division suddenly had to be withdrawn as late as 23 December, and transferred to the area north of the lower Don (Morosovskaya) to bolster the collapsed Chir front. That <u>definitely sealed the doom of Stalingrad</u>. The remaining <u>two weak panzer divisions</u>, the 17th and 23d, were not even sufficient for making a stand against the beaten enemy forces, let alone repulsing them. But also the enemy was so weakened by his extraordinary losses, including more than four hundred tanks, that he was unable to make a quick thrust against Rostov which would have cut off the entire Caucasus front.

250. We have here another example that confirms very emphatically the characteristic fighting method of the Russians: Nowhere great achievements of small units through clever leadership, but great sacrifices of stubborn masses by a flat-footed command. Only when the enemy attacked with a tenfold to twentyfold superiority could he achieve temporary successes. In the assault, however, the intellectual superiority and the individual performance of the German soldier triumphed over the clodpated concentration of enemy masses. Final success, though, was not achieved, because the emergency on another front called for the withdrawal of the decisive driving force. Before Stalingrad, too, soldierly quality fought against superior quantity.

251. The Russian higher command had assigned more than sufficient forces to prevent the relief (five corps and one main-attack army against one German panzer corps). The corps were organized very effectively, but were poorly led. If properly led, these five times superior forces would have sufficed to defeat the weak German relief force before it could launch its attack. At the very latest, however, this German corps on an unsupported forward thrust should have been attacked and beaten by the combined Russian corps when it crossed the Aksay River. But the commitment

in detail of the Russian corps enabled the very flexibly led German units to attack the individual Russian forces by surprise, and to defeat one after another. During the last days, the enemy even had to hastily form a new main-attack army and throw it against the German 6th Panzer Division in the Mishkova River sector in order to halt its further advance. This enemy army also sustained heavy losses, and would have been unable to prevent a further advance of the German armor. It had no effective tank support at all, because the decisive factor in the whole struggle, the Russian Third Tank Army, had already been beaten. The Third Tank Army was the most dangerous opponent on the route to Stalingrad. It had more than twice the number of tanks we had, and far superior antitank weapons. Its motorized troops were well trained and fought with exemplary valor. But neither numerical superiority nor valor could make up for the mistakes of the intermediate and lower commands. Only the repercussions of the great successes which the Soviet Supreme Command was able to achieve on the Chir and Don fronts caused the relief thrust to fail. An indirect but very significant role was also played by the American landing in North Africa. That landing was responsible for the fact that the armored forces stationed in France (the 6th, 7th, and 10th Panzer Divisions; and I SS Panzer Corps with the 1st, 2d, and 3d SS Panzer Divisions), which were among the crack troops of the German Army and had been brought up to full effectiveness, were not transferred as a whole to the East for fear of an American landing in southern France. Finally, after several days' hesitation, the 6th Panzer Division alone was transferred to the sector south of Stalingrad. The 7th Panzer Division followed at a later date, and arrived too late for the relief thrust. Its timely arrival would have been sufficient to carry the thrust through to its objective.

Chapter Five
RETREAT AND DELAYING ENGAGEMENTS

252. Observations of Russian fighting methods in retreat could be made particularly during the first years of the war. When the Russians had been defeated on a broad front, they re-established their broad lines only after they had retreated a considerable distance. They marched very quickly, even when retreating in extremely large numbers. Precisely at such times it was important to pursue them energetically, and to give them no opportunity for renewed resistance. The German conduct of delaying action, with leapfrog commitment of forces in successive positions, was not known to them. This method of fighting, requiring great mobility and high-grade leadership, was not used by the Russians. The Russians always sought only simple and complete solutions. When they decided to withdraw, they did so in one jump, and then immediately went over to active defense again. When armored forces which had broken through chased them off the roads, the Russians disappeared into the terrain with remarkable skill. In retreating, retiring from sight, and rapidly reassembling, the Russians were past masters. Even large forces quickly covered long distances over terrain without roads or paths. Thus, in 1941, Russian rifle regiments thrown back by our armor crossing the border at Tauroggen again opposed the same panzer division south of Leningrad, after a march of eight hundred kilometers.

253. Even if time was of the essence, the Russians succeeded in carrying off large numbers of cattle, as well as a substantial amount of equipment and supplies. They shot thousands of undesirable persons in the Baltic countries before the retreat, and carried away other tens of thousands. In retreating they did not hesitate to burn to the ground the cities and towns of their own native land, if it seemed that any advantage was to be gained (scorched-earth policy). Thus, in the retreat of 1941, they destroyed almost completely the cities of Vitebsk, Somolensk, and many others, so that nothing of value would fall into the hands of the Germans and that their advance might be delayed. All that remained for the Germans of the Russian collective farms, State farms, machine tractor stations, and manufacturing plants of all kinds, were ashes and ruins. For that reason it even became difficult in some sectors to quarter larger headquarters organizations to assure their ability to function.

254. Russian tactics of stopping or slowing down the German offensive by means of unco-ordinated counterattacks have already been treated in the preceding chapter.

Chapter Six

COMBAT UNDER UNUSUAL CONDITIONS

255. In carrying on their warfare the Russians cleverly exploited all difficulties which their country presented to the enemy. They liked to fight in villages, woods, and marshes, and in fog, rain, snow, and storm. The Russians combined the tricks of nature with their own innate cunning in order to do the greatest possible harm to the enemy.

I. <u>Fighting in Towns and Villages</u>

256. The Russians were very adept at preparing inhabited places for defense. In a short time, a village was converted into a little fortress. Wooden houses had well-camouflaged gun ports almost flush with the floor, their interiors were reinforced with sandbags or earth, observation slots were put into roofs, and bunkers built into floors and connected with adjacent houses or outside defenses by narrow trenches. The Russians blocked approach routes by well-camouflaged antitank guns or dug-in tanks. Wrecks of knocked-out tanks were specially favored for use as observation posts, or as emplacements for heavy infantry weapons, and bunkers for living quarters were dug under them. It was Russian practice to allow the enemy to draw near, and then to fire at him unexpectedly. In order to prevent heavy losses

of personnel and tanks, we had to cover the outskirts of inhabited places with artillery, tanks, or heavy weapons during the approach of our troops. Fires resulted frequently, and in many instances consumed the whole village. When the front line neared a village, the inhabitants carried their possessions into outlying woods or bunkers for safekeeping. They did not take part in the fighting of the regular troops, but served as auxiliaries, building earthworks and passing on information. The Russian practice of raiding inhabited localities during mobile warfare and of using them for other wily tactics, or converting them into strong points for defensive purposes, was responsible for the fact that numerous populated places were destroyed during combat.

257. Since the defenses on the outskirts of a locality were quickly eliminated by means of the above-mentioned German countermeasures, the Russians later led their main line of resistance right through the center of their villages, and left only a few security detachments on the outskirts facing the enemy. Permanent structures destroyed by artillery fire or aerial bombs were cleverly utilized as defense points. The ruins hid weapons and served to strengthen the underlying bunkers. Even the heaviest shelling would not drive the Russians from such positions; they had to be dislodged with hand grenades or flame throwers. The Russians upon retreating frequently burned or blasted buildings suitable for housing command posts or other important military installations. Quite often, however, the Russians left castles, former countryseats, and other spacious

dwellings intact, after they had mined the walls in a completely inconspicuous manner with <u>delayed-action bombs</u>, which were often set to explode several weeks later. These were meant to blow up entire German headquarters at one time. The possible presence of time-bombs in cities, railroad stations, bridges, and other important structures always had to be taken into account.

258. When the Russians were on the offensive, they tried to encircle fortified towns in order to bring about their fall through concentric advances. Only during major offensives would the advance forces by-pass inhabited places in order to gain ground rapidly, leaving the mopping-up to the reserves following behind. If the Russians were encircled, they defended themselves very tenaciously and capitulated only in rare cases. The large-scale battles of encirclement of 1941, when hundreds of thousands surrendered in hopeless situations after previous attempts to break out, were exceptions.

259. Fighting for the possession of villages played a still greater role in the winter. The villages blocked the few roads which had been cleared of snow, and offered warm quarters. Cleared roads and warm quarters, moreover, were the two basic prerequisites for winter warfare. Therefore, inhabited localities retained their outstanding tactical importance despite the fact that they could easily be by-passed by ski troops even in deep snow. Experience, after all, had shown that ski and sleigh forces might seriously harass the enemy, but that they would never be able to bring about major decisions. (See MS # T-36, Examples 26-29.)

260. The tactics of winter warfare therefore centered around contests for the possession of roads and inhabited places. In the East, villages and roads were infinitely more important than they were in the West or the South. In the latter theaters of war any one particular road never was a crucial factor, since the well-developed road net always offered a ready choice of alternate routes. In the East, on the other hand, the possession of one single road often was a life or death matter for an entire army. (See winter campaign 1941-42 of the Fourth Army at Moscow, MS # T-36, Example 23.) To be sure, inhabited places were tactically important in the West and South, too, and offered welcome shelter. Properly clothed, however, the troops were able to remain in the open for a long time without freezing, or even endangering their health--an impossibility in the East. The extreme tactical importance of the inhabited places during the six months of winter explains the fact that the Russians, as well as the Germans, frequently would much rather destroy them than surrender them to the enemy. Peculiarities of Russian warfare for the possession of towns and villages are also cited in numerous Examples contained in MSS # T-21, T-22, and T-36.

II. Forest Fighting

261. Forests had a magnetic attraction for the Russians. Because of their affinity to nature, the Russians were completely at home in woods, and knew how to take good advantage of them.

262. The Russians favored forests for their approach marches and as assembly areas for an attack. They came and disappeared invisibly and noiselessly through the woods. Narrow strips of woodland leading up to the outskirts of villages were used as concealed approaches by their reconnaissance patrols. They also indicated the logical course to be followed for the forward assembly prior to an attack as well as for infiltrating into German positions. Outskirts of woods were a preferred jump-off position for their mass attacks. Wave upon wave of Russians would surge out of the forests. Undaunted by the losses that the German defensive fire inflicted on their ranks, they launched the attack. Even small clearings were used for artillery firing positions. If necessary, the Russians would create such clearings by rapidly felling some trees. Quickly and cleverly they constructed positions for heavy weapons and observation posts in trees, and so were able to lend effective support to their advancing infantry. Bringing up even medium artillery and tanks through almost impenetrable forests presented no problem to the Russians.

Ex. 25 Break-Through of a Russian Tank Corps through Trackless Woodlands East of Lwow (June 1944)

263. In June 1944, Russian tanks reached a trackless forest east of Lwow through a narrow gap in our front. The whole tank corps soon followed, despite the fact that it was attacked from both flanks and heavily bombarded by artillery and rocket projectors. The Russians used their heavy KV I and KV II tanks as battering rams to crush the medium growth of timber. The attached engineers overcame some of the attendant difficulties by laying corduroy roads across the swamps, so that the infantry and artillery were soon able to follow the tanks. Just shortly before that Russian operation,

the commanders of our own panzer divisions had come to the conclusion that this forest was impenetrable even for Russian tanks. The Russian advance over this hastily improvised road, constructed with the aid of the most primitive facilities, was, for a time, accompanied by the strains of band music!

264. In an attack across open terrain with patches of forest only in its depth, the Russians endeavored to reach those patches in the shortest possible time. Forests had the same magnetic effect on the Russians as inhabited places. Whenever the Russians planned a river crossing, one could safely assume that it would take place where woods or inhabited localities reached down to the banks of the river.

Ex. 26   Forest Fighting during the Russian Break-Through Attempt across the Upper Donets (August 1943)

265. When the Russians in the course of their great counteroffensive successfully effected a break-through one hundred kilometers deep, west of Byelgorod on 5 August 1943, they seriously threatened the flanks and rear of XI Infantry Corps on the upper course of the Donets River. The enemy recognized the critical situation of the Corps and sought, by a thrust across the river, to cut its only route of retreat. In spite of heavy losses, the Russians managed to gain a foothold in a forest on the west bank of the Donets. On that occasion, a ruse paid the Russians handsome dividends. When the German local reserves immediately launched a counterthrust, they suddenly faced a Russian battalion dressed in German uniforms, and immediately ceased firing. By the time the German troops became aware of their mistake, it was already too late. The enemy took advantage of the resultant disorder, fell upon the deceived attackers, and took a large number of them prisoner. The Russians then entrenched themselves in a larger patch of woodland in order to continue their thrust from there. A counterattack, begun the next day and supported by the massed artillery of the Corps and

a rocket projector regiment, succeeded in compressing the Russians into a small area, but not in driving them back across the river, although the concentrated drum fire killed three-quarters of their forces.

266. The innate aptitudes of the Russian soldier asserted themselves to an even greater degree in defensive actions fought in forests. The Russian command was very adept at choosing and fortifying forest positions in such a way that they became impregnable after having been held a while. On the edge of woods toward the enemy, the Russians left only outposts for guarding and screening the main line of resistance, which was withdrawn deep into the forest itself. That security line also formed the springboard and the support for reconnaissance, scouting, and other operations. The main line of resistance frequently ran roughly parallel to the opposite edge of the woods and a few hundred meters inside the woods. Very extensive woods frequently concealed groups of bunkers in the central part. These bunkers, constituting an intermediate position, were to delay the advance of the enemy, deceive him as to the location of the main position, and serve as support for the outposts. The Russians also protected the exposed flanks of a forest position by groups of bunkers. Important approach routes they blocked by individual, machine-gun or antitank-gun bunkers, echeloned in depth. The immediate vicinity of the bunkers was protected by mined entanglements of branches and abatis, as well as by snipers in trees. Furthermore, the Russians used to mine all by-passes and forest glades in numerous places. These measures greatly delayed progress through a forest, because the bunkers could be

taken only after costly fighting, and because engineers had to be called upon for time-consuming mine-clearing operations. Important forward strong points in forests had facilities for all-around defense. A forester's house or a hamlet would often form the central point of the fortified position. A defense trench surrounded by obstacles and minefields completely encircled the position. The few sally ports were guarded by sentries and movable barriers. A ring of bunkers, connected with each other and with the fortress, enclosed the central point. The intermediate position was blocked by barbed wire, entanglements of branches, and mines. The previously described individual bunkers were placed along the approach routes.

267. An extensive system of bunker groups formed the <u>battle position</u> and made possible an unbroken defense of the front. In the battle position all the previously described defense expedients were found in even greater numbers. Entanglements of branches interwoven with barbed wire, and mined abatis of a depth of several hundred meters were no rarity. These obstacles prevented sudden thrusts along the roads. Wherever there might have been a possibility of bypassing these obstructions, one could be sure that mines or tank traps had been installed. In such cases the troops would often end up in a swamp or an ambush. All bunkers and defense installations were so well camouflaged that they could never be discovered by aerial reconnaissance, and by ground reconnaissance only at very close range. Because of the system of advanced strong points and security positions, it was in many cases impossible for German scouting parties

even to get close to the main defensive position. While reconnaissance in force by at least one reinforced battalion might succeed in breaking through the outer protective screen, it frequently would bog down at the supporting position of the enemy outposts. However, if the enemy gave way without offering tenacious resistance, the utmost caution was indicated since a further advance was sure to end in a prepared ambush. In such cases, entire companies repeatedly were wiped out to the last man, the prisoners being massacred.

Ex. 27   The Russian Ambush of a German Battalion near Sukhinichi (February 1942)

268. After the capture of Sukhinichi in February 1942, the 208th Infantry Division continued its northward thrust. The continuous threat from enemy forces in a woodland, as well as raids on the supply road of the Division, made it imperative that the woods be cleared of the enemy. According to reports from scouting parties, a small village occupied by a substantial number of Russians was located in the center of the woods. Since it was to be presumed that the raids were launched from that point, the Division ordered the capture of the village. Half a battalion was assigned to the task. The force was partially equipped with snowshoes and reinforced by infantry heavy weapons, which were taken along on sleds. They advanced along the road leading from Sukhinichi to the village and, having arrived at a clearing in the woods-- in the center of which lay the village--without being molested, surrounded the village. The attack met bitter resistance and failed. After having sustained heavy losses, the half-battalion retreated along its approach route. Meanwhile, enemy troops had taken up positions along the road and fell upon the retreating Germans. Only remnants of the half-battalion reached their point of origin.

269. Strongly garrisoned forest positions were difficult to attack and always cost many casualties. They were invulnerable to

attacks by the Luftwaffe, the artillery, or armor. At best, tanks and self-propelled assault guns could be employed individually or in small groups, in which case they were very useful. Very rarely could strong positions be taken if they lay deep in an extensive forest or near its far edge. Frequently whole divisions were pinned down before such positions until they could be relieved from their plight by an envelopment on the part of other forces. For that reason, forward thrusts by strong forces were not led through woods but around them, wherever such a maneuver was possible. (See MS # T-21, Example 85.)

Ex. 28   Russian Defense in Woods during the Forward Thrust from the Poretsye Bridgehead on the Luga (August 1941)

270. In the latter half of August 1941, the 6th Panzer Division was to begin a thrust toward Leningrad from the Poretsye bridgehead on the Luga River. (Ed: See App. 5.) The bridgehead was completely surrounded by woods and the sector to be attacked lay in a medium-growth, partly marshy woods with thick underbrush. The sector was occupied by the 2d and 3d Russian Proletarian Divisions. The most advanced Russian position was located about three hundred to four hundred meters ahead of the German front. The enemy trenches were narrow and deep, and had no parapets. The excavated earth had been scattered in the surrounding rank marsh grass, and the trenches themselves were so well camouflaged with branches that neither reconnaissance patrols nor aerial photography had been able to spot them during the preceding four weeks of fighting. The wire entanglements were no higher than the dense growth of grass hiding them. Single roads from the southwestern and northeastern ends of the bridgehead cut through the woods to a village beyond. The two roads were blocked by heavily wired abatis and mine fields. On the far edge of the woods a second position was located atop a sand dune, a third ran through the village, and a fourth lay behind the village. The second position was particularly well constructed. It consisted of a deep antitank ditch, in the front wall of which the enemy riflemen had

entrenched themselves, and bunkers for heavy weapons had been installed.

271. The German attack was to be launched along the abovementioned two roads. A reinforced panzer grenadier regiment, supported by strong artillery elements and a rocket projector (Werfer) battalion, advanced along each of these roads. Individual tanks were to support the engineers in the removal of the road blocks. In spite of very heavy fire concentrations on the projected points of penetration, the enemy could not be budged from his narrow, invisible zigzag trenches. To be sure, the tanks were able to reach the barriers, but the dismounted engineers were unable to remove the blocks in the defensive fire, which continued unabated. The infantry following up sought fruitlessly to find other weak spots in order to effect a breakthrough. Repulsed everywhere by the murderous defensive fire of an invisible enemy, they finally stopped, knee-deep in swampland, before the wire entanglements in front of the still unknown enemy position. Not until the following night did one company succeed in crawling forward, man by man, through the deep-cut bed of a brook which was overgrown with grass and bushes, and in infiltrating through the entanglement. That particular point had not been attacked heretofore. Strong reserves were immediately brought up. They widened the point of penetration, and cleared out the trenches and strong points of the westerly sector after hours of hand-grenade fighting. The enemy continued to maintain his position in the easterly sector. German forces could be directed against the rear of the enemy only after a thrust into the depth of the westerly sector had reached and rolled up the second position. After bitter hand-to-hand fighting the German forces were finally able to scatter the Russians also at that point, and to clear the road.

272. Only then, after a 2-day battle that exacted a heavy toll of losses from both sides, was the invisible enemy defensive system in the woods south of Ivanovskoye surmounted.

III. Fighting Around Rivers, Swamps, and Lakes

273. Military operations for the possession of rivers are

treated in a separate section of MS # T-34. It is, therefore, superfluous to discuss that subject in detail at this point. Nevertheless, it appears appropriate to point out individual peculiarities.

274. During the course of the war, the ability of the Russians to cross even the largest rivers was always a source of amazement. Rivers seemed to present no obstacle to them. When the German armies reached the Dnepr in the summer of 1941, the problem of surmounting this obstacle presented quite some difficulties to the German command, since they had no conception of the size and nature of the river. How quickly and easily this problem could be solved was demonstrated a few days later by the Russians. During the course of one night a cavalry corps crossed the river--using field expedients for ferrying men and equipment to the opposite bank, and swimming thousands of horses across--and penetrated deep into the lines of the surprised Germans.

275. Exactly two years later the German armies retiring westward made for this same river sector, and had great difficulties in reaching and crossing the Dnepr ahead of the Russians. (See MS # T-21.) By calling on all the forces and means at their disposal, the Germans had managed to occupy seven existing bridges in a sector five hundred kilometers long, but were able to establish only one float bridge and one improvised ferry because of the scarcity of ferrying equipment that prevailed by that time. On the other hand, the enemy, following in close pursuit, succeeded, even before our troops arrived, in dropping several thousand paratroops over a 350-kilometer-long part of the sector, in establishing small bridgeheads at several places, and soon thereafter in

building 57 bridges, 9 foot bridges, and other facilities for crossing the river. Thus, the Germans had a crossing over the Dnepr every 70 kilometers, the Russians one every 6 kilometers. At one ferrying point forty kilometers downstream from Kremenchug, the Russians established a small bridgehead and proceeded to ferry tanks across the river on rafts, by day and night. Their operations continued even when they were shelled by German artillery, and some of the tank-laden rafts went to the bottom of the river.

276. The Russians also made extensive use of raft bridges. These had to be built by engineers. The German engineers first learned about those bridges from the Russians and had to experiment in order to determine their load capacity. Raft bridges could be used only for crossing waters having a slow current. The raft bridge is built of tree trunks placed side by side and fastened to each other. Depending upon requirements, a second and even a third layer of logs is added, each layer being laid crosswise to the layer below. Planking, laid across the uppermost layer, serves as a roadway. The load capacity of the raft bridge can be adapted to meet existing requirements by varying the number of layers of logs. The Russians built bridges of this type ranging from a 5-ton bridge at Rogachev in 1941 to a railroad bridge of over 100 tons load capacity near Kiev in 1943. Just four days after taking Kiev, the Russians had established rail communications into the city by means of this heavy raft bridge across the Dnepr.

277. Even **swamps and lakes** were no real obstacles to the Russians as was demonstrated during the battles on the Volkhov (see MS

\# T-10), and the engagements on the Luga and Desna, as well as at many other swampy sectors.

Ex. 29 **Russian Thrust through the Pripyat Marshes toward Kowel (February 1944)**

278. When, in February 1944, a yawning gap opened on the Pripec River at the boundary between Army Group North Ukraine and Army Group Center, the Russians crossed this extensive marshy region during the muddy period with fourteen divisions, and pushed toward Kowel.

279. Several of these divisions turned south through Rowne in order to attack Lwow. Stopped near Dubno on the Ikwa River by the Fourth Panzer Army, they vainly tried to take the few strongly manned crossings over the extensive swamps on both sides of the river. Nevertheless, one morning a Russian battalion appeared in the rear of Dubno. It was surrounded by armor and captured. Interrogation of the prisoners revealed that during the night the enemy riflemen had crawled on their bellies across the slightly frozen marsh, which was up to six hundred meters wide and could not be crossed on foot, and arrived exhausted and covered with muck.

Ex. 30 **Naked Russian Infantrymen Cross a Lake under cover of Darkness and Launch an Attack (September 1943)**

280. In September 1943, the XI Infantry Corps stood on the Dnepr astride Kremenchug, and had to protect its right wing against the enemy who had broken through in the adjacent sector. A shallow lake, four kilometers long and from three hundred to five hundred meters wide, facilitated the flank protection. The western bank was guarded by weak German forces. One night they suddenly were attacked and driven back by from six hundred to eight hundred Russians. Under cover of darkness these Russians had waded across a shallow spot of the marshy lake without a stitch of clothing, and--equipped only with small arms and ammunition-- had surprised the German security. Only quickly brought up mobile reserves were able to encircle the Russians and take them prisoner.

IV. Fighting in Darkness and Inclement Weather

281. The Russians used darkness and fog primarily for troop movements, preparations for attack, construction of field fortifications, and supply operations. Reconnaissance in force, and raids likewise were usually carried out under cover of darkness or hazy weather. In these instances, the Russians proceeded with Asiatic patience, cunning, and perseverance. Not infrequent were Russian night attacks in strength of up to a regiment.

282. In the Arctic, we encountered commando teams specially trained in Byelomorsk for night raids into our rear area. Appropriate to the nature of their mission, these troops were equipped only with absolutely essential items. Minutely detailed orders took care of every phase of the undertaking, and were carried out methodically and to the letter. Here, too, the Russians proved themselves fearless fighters. As in other regions, attacks on strong points in the Arctic were broken off only when the Russian casualties amounted to many times the strength of the strong-point complements.

Ex. 31   A Siberian Rifle Division Breaks Through the German Lines at Uzlovaya under cover of Darkness (November 1941)

283. One of the planned night attacks was that of a Siberian Division against the 112th Infantry Division southeast of Uzlovaya toward the end of November 1941. (Ed: See App. 6.) After it had finished unloading, the Siberian Division advanced on the 112th Infantry Division early in the night. Having gained a substantial amount of territory to the north beyond Bogoroditsk in minor engagements during the previous day, the 112th Division had bivouacked for the night. About twenty tanks led the Siberian

attack. The mere appearance by night of tanks in front of the lines of the 112th Division produced a severe shock. No means of defense were at hand for the time being. At that, any defenses would have had only a local effect at night. When the attacking Siberians now appeared behind the tanks, complete panic broke out. The elements of the 112th Division hit by the attack fell back many kilometers, close up to the northern outskirts of Bogoroditsk. Special steps had to be taken to restore control of the situation. The territorial gains of the Siberian division remained limited to a few kilometers; a large-scale exploitation of their success did not follow. The Russians probably had reached their objective and had not planned any further advance.

284. Night attacks on a major scale, however, remained the exception to the rule. The Russians undertook such attacks only when they had orders from a higher command, or when they had failed to take an important objective in a day attack in spite of a mass commitment of men and equipment. They were generally acts of desperation, where everything was staked on one card. Examples were the night tank battle near Morozovskaya (See MS # T-36, Example 33), and the night attack of the Russian Fifth Tank Army on Kharkov in the summer of 1943 (Example 20).

285. During the polar winter only small-scale warfare was possible, which, however, the Russians as well as the Germans waged zealously. Security and reconnaissance activity had to be greatly increased. Surprise attacks were always to be expected because it remained dark throughout the day. The generally known principles of defense against night operations held true under those conditions. About the only new feature was the fact that fighting was not limited

MS # T-22   -143-

to mere local actions, for raiding parties consisting of smaller units did not hesitate to thrust far into the depths of the enemy front (the Russians to the Turku- and Helsinki-Petsamo highway (Eismeerstrasse), the Germans to the Murmansk railroad). Both sides frequently employed specially trained troops in these operations. The Russians used troops trained in Byelomorsk; the Germans used special Finnish units.

<u>Ex. 32</u>

<u>App. 12</u>

286. Night surprise attacks of another type were the attempts at <u>breaking out of pockets</u>, such as took place in 1941 at <u>Maloryta</u>, <u>Vyazma</u>, <u>Bryansk</u>, and other encirclements. Here, the Russians made no long preparations, but hurled themselves into the open in tightly packed hordes at whatever points they believed there was a chance of getting through. At Maloryta, however, it was strange how the Russians, after a successful break-out of part of their forces, spent thirty-six hours in encircling and storming a village still held by the Germans. This village was in the rear of the Russians, and by their operation they lost the advantage of their nighttime break-out. At that, possession of the village would have been completely unimportant for the success of the break-out. Their orders, however, probably read that way.

287. In this connection it might be mentioned that the commander of the army group at Bryansk, General Petrov, was killed on 18 October 1941 in a night attempt to break out of the Bryansk pocket. The adjutant of the reconnaissance battalion of the 56th German Infantry Division, which had taken up a position in front of the attempted break-through on the eastern side of the pocket, suddenly heard several shots in the night; it so happened that those shots had no connection with Petrov. The adjutant with his runners, machine pistols slung about their necks, hurried in the direction of the shots and suddenly saw a file of men moving along the edge of a clearing in the woods. He shouted, "Stoy!" At the same moment the leader of the file aimed the machine pistol hanging down his chest at the adjutant, but before he could pull the trigger, the adjutant fired. The leader was killed.

instantly, and the next man fell to the ground, seriously wounded. The leader was General Petrov; the second man, Major of State Security, Shabalin.

288. Russian large-scale offensive always started by daylight. Usually the early morning hours were chosen. H hour remained the same even if dense fog obscured everything all day long, as, for instance, at the beginning of the second battle of East Prussia on 14 January 1945.

289. It was, however, highly advantageous to attack heavily fortified Russian strong points, antitank-gun and tank fronts by night. Attempts to take them by day would have cost large numbers of lives. Night attacks were almost always successful when carried out by troops specially trained for this type of combat, and usually cost only a few casualties.

Ex. 33   Failures of Russian Defense in Night Operations (1942-43)

290. In the spring of 1943, during the war of position north of Tomarovka, an assault detachment in company strength of the 167th Infantry Division succeeded in infiltrating the Russian front by night, raiding a strongly garrisoned village from the rear, and driving the enemy out. During the previous day, two battalions had been unable to take the village despite strong artillery support.

291. In January 1943 a company of the 6th Panzer Division supported by six self-propelled assault guns was similarly able to take an important fortified village north of Tatsinskaya by a night assault from the rear. Previously, a panzer grenadier regiment and a 60-tank panzer battalion of the neighboring division had vainly endeavored all day to take this village.

292. Verkhniy-Kumskiy, the bitterly contested keypoint of

Russian defense against the German relief thrust on Stalingrad, also was taken in a night attack by a panzer grenadier battalion with but minor losses.

293. Even the Russians began no far-reaching operations in really <u>bad weather</u>; but such weather suited them very well for local operations. During fog and blizzards the Russians always developed lively reconnaissance activity and raided advanced security posts. Not infrequently would the Russians attack in battalion or regimental strength during driving thundershowers, in order to effect reconnaissance in force, to improve their position, or to gain a favorable jump-off position for a major offensive. In winter they exploited the cold eastern storms of the steppes for such assaults, especially in the southern sector. On those occasions the Russians often succeeded in entering the German trenches without firing a shot, and in taking many prisoners. Indeed, the Russians knew very well that the easterly gales drove such clouds of powdered snow ahead of them that the German soldiers were unable to observe and take aim against the wind. They were, therefore, practically defenseless. Only by a ruse were the German divisions fighting there able to regain mastery of the situation. Those front sectors particularly threatened during the easterly gales were simply evacuated, and the forces quartered in the villages situated along the sides of the gaps. When the Russians rushed forward into, or over the empty trenches, the German forces wheeled against the rear of the Russians and attacked them from the east; the Russians were then just as defenseless as the Germans had previously been.

The Russian attacks, too, ended in captivity. As a result, the Russians later ceased attacking during easterly gales.

Chapter Seven
CAMOUFLAGE, DECEPTION, AND PROPAGANDA

294. Camouflage, deception, and propaganda were expedients much used by the Russians. They, too, reflected in every aspect the oriental character of the people. The Russians carried out measures conforming to their natural talents, such as camouflage and deception, with great skill and effectiveness. Their front propaganda, however, was crude and naive for the most part. Because it did not correspond to the psychology and mentality of the German soldier in any way, it was ineffective. Although pursued zealously, and with a great variety of media, it attained no appreciable success up to the end of the war for precisely those reasons.

I. <u>Camouflage</u>

295. The Russians were excellent at camouflage. With their primitive instinct they understood perfectly how to blend into their surroundings, and were trained to vanish into the ground upon even the slightest provocation. As previous Examples have illustrated, they skillfully used darkness, vegetation, and bad weather for concealing their intentions. Their movements at night and their advances through wooded terrain were carried out with exemplary quietness. Now and then they would communicate with each other by means of cleverly imitated animal cries.

296. Noteworthy, too, was the camouflage of river crossings by the construction of <u>underwater bridges</u>, which were frequently employed by the Russians. For this purpose they used a submersible underwater bridging gear, which could be submerged or raised by flooding or pumping out the compartments. The deck of the bridge was usually about thirty centimeters below water level, and was thus shielded from aerial observation.

297. Artificial camouflage was another device not unknown to the Russians. Even at the beginning of the war we came across Russian troops wearing camouflage suits of bast fibers dyed green. Lying prone in the grass, these soldiers could be spotted only at a very short distance, and frequently were passed by without having been noticed at all. Reconnaissance patrols frequently wore "leaf" suits of green cloth patches, which provided excellent camouflage in the woods. Russians wearing face masks were no rarity.

298. The Russians enforced strict <u>camouflage discipline</u>. Any man who left his shelter during the day was punished very severely, if it was forbidden for reasons of camouflage. In this way the Russians were able to conceal the presence of large units even in winter, as the following example illustrates.

Ex. 34   <u>Successful Concealment of the First Russian Tank Army at Vinnitsa (January 1944)</u>

299. In January 1944 the First Russian Tank Army attempted to take the important railroad hub of Zhmerinka in a surprise attack. The attack was repulsed, and the Army encircled to the southeast of Vinnitsa. It broke out of the encirclement during the very first

night, and disappeared. The bulk of this Russian army escaped completely unnoticed through the gaps left by the insufficient forces engaged in the encirclement. In spite of deep snow and clear weather, it could not even be determined in which direction the enemy forces had escaped. From the situation, it was to be assumed that they had hidden in the immediate vicinity in a group of numerous, rather large villages with extensive, adjoining orchards. Since our own armored units had previously driven through those villages, the tank tracks gave no reliable evidence that they were hiding there. For two days and nights the Luftwaffe scouted for the whereabouts of the Tank Army, and in this connection took excellent aerial photographs of the entire area in which the villages were located. But neither aerial observation nor the study of aerial photographs provided any clue. Not until the third day, when a strong German tank force pushed into the group of villages, was the hiding place of the entire First Russian Tank Army established in that very area. All tanks and other vehicles had been excellently camouflaged in barns, under sheds, straw piles, haystacks, piles of branches, etc.; and all movement during the day had been forbidden, so that nothing gave away their presence.

II. Deception

300. Prior to offensives the Russian made extensive use of deception. In order to mislead the enemy as to the time and place of impending large-scale offensives, the Russians faked concentrations in other sectors by preparing a great number of fire positions for artillery, mortars, and rocket projectors. They strengthened this impression by moving smaller bodies of troops into those sectors by day and night, as well as by setting up dummy artillery pieces, tanks, and aircraft, and making appropriate tracks leading up to them. The Russians also were known to place an entire tank army behind an unimportant sector, so as

to create the false impression of an impending attack from that point. By running their motors at night they sought to create the impression that tank and motorized columns were on the move. Artillery trial fire and the use of roving guns likewise were among the most commonly used Russian deception practices. Despite the full use of various methods of deception, however, the time and place of Russian large-scale attacks could accurately be determined in nearly all instances.

301. For purposes of deception on a more limited scale, the Russians frequently used German uniforms for whole units (see Example 26) as well as for individuals. That method of deception was almost always successful.

<u>Ex. 35</u>   Deception by Individuals (1943-44)

302. In the summer of 1943 a German-speaking Russian in the uniform of a German officer succeeded in driving a German truck right up to headquarters of the Rowne military government detachment (Ortskommandantur), and in obtaining an audience with the commandant, a general. He gagged the commandant, wrapped him up in a big rug, carried him out to the truck which he had left idling outside, and delivered him to the partisans. Only by the words, "Thanks, comrade"--words that an officer in the German Army simply would not use in addressing a private--did he arouse the suspicion of the kidnapped officer's orderly, who had innocently helped him load the heavy carpet into the truck. An immediate report by the orderly cleared up the mysterious incident, but did not lead to the apprehension of the kidnapper.

303. In Lwow, in the spring of 1944, apparently the very same Russian, dressed as a German officer, succeeded by means of similar trickery in shooting to death the deputy governor of Galicia as well as a lieutenant colonel, and later a sentinel who wanted to inspect his truck. Each time he succeeded in escaping.

MS # T-22   -151-

304. Similar surprise raids and deceptions of combat troops through the misuse of German uniforms occurred at all sectors of the front in ever increasing numbers. It would take too long to describe the countless examples within the framework of this study.

III. Propaganda

305. The propaganda of the Russians exploited military and political problems. All the technical means by which modern propaganda is disseminated were used: radio, press, leaflets, photographs, planes flying by night towing illuminated streamers or equipped with loud speakers and phonographs, loudspeakers set up on the ground, leaflet shells, rumors spread by agents, Russian PWs, and Germans pretending to have escaped from Russian captivity. Since there were also Finnish troops on the Arctic Front, to whom different things were of importance, the enemy propaganda at that front sometimes met with difficulties, and was not properly co-ordinated. One also had to differentiate between propaganda aimed at higher military commanders, the troops, and the German people. These various groups to be propagandized were dealt with and approached from entirely different angles. From a literary and artistic standpoint, much of the Russian propaganda was of high caliber.

306. The Russian intelligence service covered events in the German Army with amazing speed and accuracy. Photographs, for example, taken by one of our own propaganda companies for various reasons, appeared almost simultaneously in the pertinent Russian army newspapers.

The propaganda at the front, however, was crude and clumsy. For that reason, it made but little impression. Political and military satire was used a great deal.

307. Information on Russian propaganda addressed to their own troops was obtained from captured Russian army newspapers. It, too, employed words and pictures. Nationalism and ideological fanaticism were exploited with equal intensity. The Russians seemed to criticize quite frankly some of the events at the front. Conditions among German troops in opposing positions were treated satirically for the most part. In the propaganda directed at their own front lines, the Russians pounded into their soldiers' heads the fairy tale that the Germans shot every PW on the spot. This propaganda-induced fear of being taken prisoner was to make the Russian soldiers stand their ground to the very end. The fairy tale was believed, and that particular line of propaganda accomplished its purpose. There were only relatively few Russian deserters. On the other hand, older Russian soldiers who had worked in Germany as prisoners during World War I deserted very frequently. They were immune to the atrocity stories.

308. The Russian command was worried that its propaganda of lies would be unmasked and rendered ineffective by the civilian population in reconquered areas, a goodly proportion of whom had become friendly to the Germans. For that reason they forbade the quartering of troops in villages located in such areas. Even in winter the soldiers were forbidden to enter those villages.

309. A large part of the Russian propaganda effort was

devoted to studying and counteracting German propaganda activities. Reading and passing on of German propaganda leaflets was forbidden under penalty of death.

310. By erecting signs, by loudspeaker messages, or by dropping propaganda leaflets from aircraft, the Russians made extensive use of front-line propaganda urging the Germans to surrender or desert. Often the commander was addressed personally, sometimes by captured German officers of all ranks, who allegedly belonged to the "Free Germany" organization. Many propaganda leaflets were dropped that represented pictorially the Russian superiority in men, weapons, and materiel, as well as in armament potential. Also alleged German atrocities and acts of destruction were shown. These pictures had been posed so unskillfully that even a layman would immediately recognize them to be forgeries. It was, however, not quite clear just what propaganda purpose the exhibition of nude women standing on the breastworks of Russian trenches was supposed to accomplish. They supposedly were German girls who had fallen into Russian hands.

311. Neither the spoken nor the printed Russian propaganda inspired any credulity, for it contained too many <u>obvious lies</u>. Besides, the German soldier had seen the dubious blessings of Bolshevism at close range, and had discussed this dictatorial system with its opponents among the Russian people. There were a great many anti-Bolsheviks among the intellectual circles. Those people voluntarily joined in the German retreat in 1943, because they wanted to have nothing more to do with the Russian system.

312. Even before the Eastern Campaign, strong anti-German propaganda was disseminated. In the schools of many Russian cities and villages we found German language texts which contained the most coarse, insulting invectives aimed at Germany. That was the manner in which Communism spiritually prepared for war against Germany and poisoned the minds of the Russian people. In a fairly large village south of Leningrad, half-grown, German-speaking boys naively admitted that they had been selected as Komsomoltsy (the Soviet counterpart of the German Hitler Youth) for Magdeburg.

313. Occasionally the Russians also doubled back German PWs with false reports. We frequently picked up particularly well-trained Russian deserters who were supposed to supply us with false intelligence. This type of propaganda was somewhat less than a success. With the exception of individual foreign soldiers in German uniform, instances of desertion from the German ranks remained limited to the acts of a few desperadoes. Nor did the so-called Seydlitz Propaganda have any effect.

314. During the first years of the war the Russians apparently had sought to impress the German troops and lower their morale by committing numerous atrocities against them. The great number of such crimes, committed on all sectors of the front especially in 1941-1942, but also during later German counteroffensives, tends to support that presumption.

Ex. 36   Atrocities as a Medium of Propaganda (1941-43)

315. On 25 June 1941, two batteries of the 267th Infantry Division near Milniki (Army Group Center) were overrun in the course of a Russian night break-through and bayonetted to the last man. Individual dead bore up to 17 bayonet wounds, among them even holes through the eyes.

316. On 26 August 1941, while combing a woods for enemy forces, a battalion of the 465th Infantry Regiment was attacked from all sides by Russian tree snipers, and lost seventy-five dead and twenty-five missing. In a follow-up thrust, all of the missing men were found shot through the neck.

317. In January 1942, an SS division attacked the area north of Szyczewka (Army Group Center). On that occasion, a battalion fighting in a dense forest area suffered a reverse and lost 26 men. German troops who later penetrated to that point found all the missing SS men massacred. In April 1942, an elderly Russian civilian, a carpenter, appeared at a German division headquarters southwest of Rzhev, and reported that he had encountered a group of about forty German PWs with a Russian escort in his village a few kilometers behind the Russian front. The prisoners, he continued, had soon afterward been halted at the northern outskirts of the village, where they had dug deep pits. According to eyewitness reports, the prisoners had subsequently been shot, and buried in those pits. A few days later, the village was captured in a German thrust. The incident was investigated, and found to be true.

318. During the battle of Zhizdra, in early March 1943, a battalion of the 590th Grenadier Regiment was assigned the mission of mopping up a sector overgrown with brush. The attack failed. When, on 19 March 1943, the sector again passed into German hands after a counterattack by the corps, forty corpses of soldiers from the battalion were found with their eyes gouged out, or their ears, noses, and genitals cut off. Corpses found in another sector of the battlefield bore signs of similar mutilations. The news of these atrocities gave rise to a feeling of hate among our own troops and strengthened their power of resistance. Only in the weaklings did it awaken fear of falling into Russian hands.

319. On 5 July 1943, during the German pincers attack on Kursk (Operation ZITADELLE), a battalion on the

southern flank of the 320th Infantry Division lunged forward without being supported by other units. It ran head-on into the counterattack of an enemy division, and was repulsed. About 150 men were taken prisoner. Shortly thereafter we monitored a telephone conversation between a Russian lower and higher headquarters (probably regiment and division), which went about as follows:

Regimental commander: "I have 150 Fritzes (derogatory term for German soldiers) here. What shall I do with them?"

Division commander: "Keep a few for interrogation, and have the others liquidated."

In the evening of the same day, the presumed regimental commander reported the order executed, stating that the majority of the Fritzes had been <u>killed</u> immediately, and the remainder after they <u>had been</u> interrogated.

320. The Russians sought to intimidate their own civilian population by means of similar atrocities.

In March 1943, after the recapture of Zolochev, a small city thirty-five kilometers north of Kharkov, the inhabitants told the German military police that the Russians, before their retreat, had herded and whipped a rather large number of local boys between the ages of fourteen and seventeen years naked through the streets in intense cold. Afterward, they were said to have disappeared into the firehouse, where the NKVD had its headquarters, never to be seen again. During a subsequent search, all of the missing boys were found in a deep cellar of the firehouse, shot through the neck and covered with horse manure. The bodies were identified and claimed by relatives. All had severely frostbitten limbs. The reason for this particular atrocity was assumed to have been the alleged aid rendered the German occupation forces.

321. One medium of propaganda employed very frequently by the Russians during the last years of the war were German PWs who would be <u>doubled back</u> to the German lines, usually to sectors held by their

own regiments, with the mission of inducing their comrades to desert by telling them how well they would be treated as Russian prisoners. That type of propaganda failed, as did similar attempts on the part of the Germans with Russian PWs who had volunteered for this assignment.

322. Few Russian soldiers, on the other hand, believed <u>German propaganda</u>. Whenever it fell on fertile soil, its effects were promptly neutralized by means of counterpropaganda and coercion. Except during the great encirclement operations, there were only isolated instances of wholesale desertion of Russian units. If it did occur, or if the number of individual deserters increased, the Soviet commissars immediately took drastic countermeasures.

<u>Ex. 37</u>   <u>Desertion of an Uzbek Company (Byelgorod, 1943)</u>

323. During a protracted period of position warfare along the upper course of the Donets in the spring of 1943, a front-line unit of XI Infantry Corps south of Byelgorod was able to take a large number of prisoners. To begin with, those prisoners were taken in midday raids, since it had been ascertained from deserters that the Russians in this terrain sector—which could be readily observed from the western bank of the river—were allowed to move only at night, and therefore slept during the day. The prisoners, moreover, admitted that many of their comrades were dissatisfied and would like to desert. However, they were afraid of being fired upon by the Germans and would have difficulties crossing the deep river to the German lines. Contact with the company of malcontents was soon established, and the necessary arrangements made. Unobtrusive light signals on the chosen night informed the Russian company that the necessary ferrying equipment was ready, and that German weapons stood ready to cover their crossing. All necessary precautions had been taken in case of a Russian ruse. Just the same, the company really dribbled down to the banks of the river, and in several trips was ferried across the

Donets in rubber boats; the company commander, an Uzbek first lieutenant, being the very first. Part of the company, however, ran into Russian mine fields, suffering considerable losses from exploding mines as well as from the fire of the alerted Russian artillery.

The result of this undertaking and the above-mentioned incidents was that, having become unreliable, the 15th Uzbek Division was immediately withdrawn from the front, disciplined, and committed elsewhere.

324. Other successful, improvised media of front propaganda are mentioned in MS # T-21, Examples 89 and 90.

THE RED AIR FORCE

CONTENTS

	Page
Chapter One – A LUFTWAFFE EVALUATION	162
Chapter Two – A GROUND FORCE EVALUATION	166
I. Tactical Employment	166
II. Combat Techniques	171

Chapter One

A LUFTWAFFE EVALUATION

325. Numerically, the Red Air Force was greatly underestimated by the Germans before the beginning of the Eastern Campaign. In spite of its numerical strength, which increased considerably during the course of the war, it had no decisive influence on the outcome of the battles in the East.

326. <u>Russian air force tactics</u> were inflexible and strictly followed a fixed pattern. They were wanting in adaptability. Only in late 1944 and early 1945 could the first beginnings of strategic air warfare be observed. The Russian Long Range Force (Fernkampffliegerkorps), which came under the surveillance of our radio intelligence as early as 1941, was employed primarily in transport operations. Although the Russian Air Force was an independent service of the armed forces, it was employed almost exclusively on the battlefield, in joint operations with the Army.

327. Impending Russian attacks would be detected by—among other clues—the early assembly and concentration of combat aviation on airfields near the front. In this connection, the Russians proved very adept at building auxiliary airfields. Ruthlessly exploiting labor forces drawn from the civilian population, and using the most primitive equipment, they would have the airfields completed and ready for take-offs within an amazingly short time. Neither winter nor the mud-

dy periods interfered with their work.

328. The Russian Air Force made liberal use of dummy airfields and aircraft, as well as of numerous methods of camouflage.

329. In combat, the direction and commitment of aviation was assumed by command posts near the front, one of the most ably handled phases in this respect being the control of fighter aircraft from the ground. On the other hand, co-operation between fighter and ground-attack aircraft or bomber formations left much to be desired. Fighter escorts seldom accompanied them on their missions; if they did, they scattered upon first contact with the enemy.

330. The Russians proved to be excellent bad-weather pilots. Although not equipped for instrument flying, fighters and ground-attack aircraft hedge-hopped over battlefields in the most inclement weather. They liked to take advantage of low ceilings and blizzards in order to surprise the enemy.

331. Russian night fighters as a rule confined themselves to attacks on those targets on which they had been briefed, and were equipped with only the most basic navigation aids. One amazing thing was that Russian night fighters almost always flew with their position lights burning.

332. Air force formations concentrated for major operations always revealed a rapid decline of fighting potential once they had joined action. The number of planes capable of flying combat missions decreased rapidly, and a rather long time was required to restore them to flying condition. The Russians made extended use of artificial

smoke for camouflaging and protecting industrial plants, railroad junctions, and bridges against strategic air attacks.

333. The rapid repair of bomb damage was noteworthy, especially in the case of railroad installations. Again, labor forces for this purpose were ruthlessly commandeered from the civilian population.

334. Air supply operations for partisans assumed substantial proportions during the course of the war. Planes either landed the supplies, or dropped them by parachute. Agents and armed saboteurs dropped behind the German lines likewise played a special role.

335. At the beginning of the war, the ground troops were extremely vulnerable to air attack. Very soon, however, a change took place. Russian troops became tough and invulnerable to attacks by Stukas and ground-attack aircraft.

Training in defense against low-level attacks was well handled. Every weapon was unhesitatingly turned against the attacking aircraft, thereby constituting a formidable defense. Whenever possible, the Russian troops avoided billets and concealed themselves masterfully in the terrain. If, in exceptional cases, they sought shelter in inhabited places, they had strict orders not to show themselves outdoors in the daytime.

336. In keeping with Soviet ideology, the Russians employed an increasing number of female pilots and other female air crew members as the war went on. Women not only flew transport missions, but manned combat planes as well.

337. In conclusion, it may be said that the Red Air Force,

although conceived and built up on a large scale, was very primitively trained. Its will to fight, its aggressive spirit, and its mastery of technical aspects left much to be desired. Although constantly superior in numbers to the Luftwaffe, it was always inferior when it came to combat. Usually a small number of German fighters sufficed to clear the skies of Russian planes.

Chapter Two

A GROUND FORCE EVALUATION

I. <u>Tactical Employment</u>

338. With regard to materiel and training, the Soviet Air Force was always much inferior to the Luftwaffe despite the fact that the number of its planes increased steadily, and had outnumbered those of the Luftwaffe as early as 1942. Not even the introduction of new Russian types of planes was able to effect any decisive change in the disproportionate performances of the belligerents. For that reason, the Russian Air Force often was no factor at all in ground warfare. Sometimes it played a secondary role, and never one so decisive as that of the air forces of the Western Allies.

339. At the beginning of the great German offensive in the East, the ground troops saw only flights of three or four reconnaissance planes, individual bomber squadrons, and only a few fighters (Rata*). They quickly became victims of German fighters. Seldom did

---
*Ed: The Soviet I-16 single-seat pursuit plane. First dubbed the "<u>Rata</u>" in the Spanish Civil War.
---

one of the reconnaissance planes return from a mission. No sooner had they been sighted than a long trail of smoke told of their annihilation. Their crews followed them down in parachutes, they being among the first Russian prisoners who with bitter hate, or, in individual cases, with uncontrolled sobbing, awaited their fate: they expected to be shot, as their propaganda had led them to believe. They became all the more confused when we treated them in a friendly manner, even as guests. The same thing happened to the bombers which flew straight toward their targets, without fighter escorts, in single squadrons of five or six planes, or in from two to three squadrons, one right behind the other. They did not change their course even when the powerful German Flak played havoc with them. Direct hits frequently tore planes into shreds. The rest of the squadron would continue toward its objective until it was shot down by German fighters during the bombing run or the return flight. It happened repeatedly that a whole squadron would be shot down in a few minutes. At that time, an attack by Russian bombers meant nothing more to the ground troops than an exciting spectacle, which always ended in tragedy for the Russians. Not until the Russians had realized the futility of their efforts did they attempt to ward off their fate by jettisoning their bombs and quickly turning tail upon the approach of German fighters. In that way at least some of their planes succeeded in reaching the home base, only to be that much more certain of being finished off the next day.

340. The Russians were in a fair way to lose their last aircraft by this completely futile <u>commitment in detail</u>. True, the Russian Air Force was able to replace the lost planes, but it never did recover from the shock effect of the German fighters. The Russian fear of German fighters was evident right up to the end of the war.

341. Soon, however, the bloody lessons began to bear first

fruit. During the battles on the frontier, the Russian planes could be neutralized almost completely, but later, when the German troops were crossing the Dnepr and Dvina Rivers, concentrations of bomber units with fighter escorts did make their presence felt. Skillfully maneuvering, they hit the bridges and crossing sites in surprise attacks; coming in from the flanks or from the rear they harassed the German troops crossing the rivers, and were responsible for our first losses. However, the German crossings of the two rivers were not delayed, let alone stopped. At the Luga the Russians employed their new technique by using all aircraft available in the Leningrad area in shuttle raids, in order to destroy individual, isolated bridgeheads of advanced German armored elements. We suffered considerable losses, because our troops were squeezed into a narrow area, and no air support was to be had for countering the Russians due to the fact that the ground organization of the Luftwaffe had not yet caught up. Nevertheless, the tactical effect was nil, for the Russian Air Force carried on its own private war, as did the artillery, the tanks, and the infantry; of the latter, each division attacked in detail (see Example 14). The result was that in July 1941, for example, the Russian forces, eight to ten times superior in strength to the Germans, were not able to take the Poretsye bridgehead (110 kilometers southwest of Leningrad), which had been cut off completely during the first days. The fact that the Russians did not succeed in destroying even one of two wooden bridges that were located within three hundred meters of each other, after bombing them daily for a period of weeks, and sending two thousand heavy shells in their direction every day, attested to the meager technical skill of the artillery and the bombers.

342. The lack of any co-operation between the various arms of the service, and the deficiency in technical skill, led to continuous failures in the above-mentioned sector as well as on all other fronts. The Russians, though, gradually began to recognize these mistakes, too, and obviously strove for improvement. In fact, they developed appreciable technical skill. Co-operation between the combined arms also improved visibly. Nevertheless, this particular aspect remained their weakness to the end of the war. The art of co-operation presupposed a measure of personal initiative, knowledge of tactics, and acute perceptory faculties, that the Russian did not possess because those qualities ran counter to his national character and his upbringing. He attempted to compensate for those serious weaknesses by means of <u>mass commitments</u> of forces and materiel also in the case of his air force. In the air, however, his efforts were not crowned with the same degree of success as on the ground. The ground forces finally won the laurels of victory even without decisive support from the air force. At any rate, the endeavor on the part of the air force led to the formation of main efforts which became more pronounced from year to year, and which made themselves felt all the more during the Russian large-scale offensives of the last war years, when the fighting strength of the Luftwaffe was ebbing visibly because of the fuel shortage and the grievous losses in other theaters.

343. The Russian Air Force missed its first great chance

in the winter of 1941-42 when the Germans were withdrawing before Moscow. A concentration of most of its air power on the German columns, confined to the few roads that were free from snow, would have had a devastating effect (See MS # T-36, Example 23).

344. Even during the great Russian offensive in the winter of 1942-43 between the Don and the lower course of the Dnepr, as well as during the defense against the German relief push on Stalingrad, the concentrations of Russian aircraft were as yet not strong enough to influence the course of events to any appreciable extent. Air operations properly co-ordinated as to time and place with those of the ground forces were likewise an exception to the rule.

345. As of the summer of 1943, on the other hand, the concentrations of Russian planes were much greater and their activity much more vigorous. The Russian Air Force played an important role in the battle south of Kursk (the German ZITADELLE attack, July 1943) and in the Russian counteroffensive in August 1943. But its activity soon dwindled to the extent that a month later the German armies succeeded in escaping across the few Dnepr bridges to a position behind the river barrier without any interference on the part of the Russian Air Force. (See MS # T-21, Example 69.)

346. Similar mass sorties were repeated in the battle of Lwow and Vitebsk in 1944, and in the second battle of East Prussia in 1945. The main efforts, however, though clearly recognizable at the start, always dissolved within a short time, and the Russian Air Force disappeared.

II. Combat Techniques

347. At the start of the war, missions were flown at high altitudes. Fighters (Rata) attacking at <u>low level</u> were first encountered on the northern front at the Luga River. They strafed and dropped small bombs on batteries or marching columns, without accomplishing any noteworthy results. During the break-through of the Leningrad Line in September 1941, there appeared for the first time small groups of Russian fighters equipped with <u>rocket bombs</u>. Their accuracy and effectiveness was inconsequential.

348. The IL-2, a very effective and unpleasant <u>ground-attack</u> plane made its debut in February 1943. It could be identified by a cockpit armored with bulletproof glass about 100-mm. thick. The pilot was protected by steel plates in the rear and bottom of the cockpit. That type airplane was invulnerable to rifle and machine-gun fire of any caliber. Its armor also withstood 20-mm. Flak projectiles. It is, therefore, understandable that these ground-attack aircraft were used at danger points, and unceasingly harassed ground troops once they had caught them in a low-level attack. In that manner they were able to bring daylight movements of motorized troops to a standstill, and to inflict considerable losses on them with their twin-barreled machine-gun fire and small fragmentation bombs. Flak guns of 37-mm. or heavier caliber were of no use in the defense against their hedge-hopping attacks, because they flew too fast for allowing proper aim. Thus, there was nothing to do but to use the 20-mm. armor-piercing ammunition, the use of which had been forbidden for any other purpose than antitank

defense. As is illustrated in MS # T-36, Example 35, they suffered such heavy losses once we used the special-purpose ammunition for the 20-mm. Flak, that they immediately disappeared from the scene.

349. By the winter of 1944-45, Russian antitank weapons in aircraft had become so highly developed that they represented a seriously growing menace to tanks and self-propelled assault guns. By January 1945, for example, during the second battle of East Prussia, as many as eight self-propelled assault guns were set afire on one particular day by Russian antitank planes.

350. That year, too, the Russians began to hunt down locomotives, and individual motor vehicles which they suspected of carrying senior officers.

The <u>locomotive hunts</u> led to serious losses on individual railroad lines located close to the front. The losses ceased only after the trains on those lines had been armed with light Flak. On the Arctic front, the destruction of locomotives had particularly troublesome consequences. Since the Finnish supply of locomotives was very limited the Finnish Railroad Ministry wanted to discontinue operations on the Kemijaervi line, which was seriously endangered but urgently needed for German supply operations.

The hunting of individual motor vehicles also led to losses. On Easter Sunday 1944, for example, an army commander was traveling to the front north of Buczacz, Galicia, when Russian fighter squadrons attacked his car. They made repeated runs on the lone automobile, killed the commander's entourage, blew the car to bits with eighty bombs, and prevented the commander himself from continuing his journey. Only when the higher commanders used old, nonidentified cars did the attacks cease.

351. Russian <u>daytime bombing raids</u> were even in the later years of the war carried out mostly by smaller groups at altitudes of two thousand meters or higher. Raids by whole wings were an exception to the rule. Carpet bombing by large bomber formations was unknown to the Russians. On the other hand, during the last two war years, they frequently dropped clusters of small fragmentation bombs on live targets. The bombs would fall within a radius of a hundred meters in such a dense pattern that no living object within the effective beaten zone could escape the splinters. The bombs fell into even the narrowest trenches and, because of their great fragmentation, were very dangerous and greatly feared. German planes surprised on the ground often would be set afire or destroyed by the fragments of bombs dropped in such patterns. The effect of these bombs on the morale of the troops was likewise very considerable.

352. The Soviet bombers displayed poor <u>marksmanship</u>. For example, in a two-fold attempt to help their sorely pressed infantry on the edge of a forest by bombing the German lines, all the bombs fell on the Russian position and wreaked such havoc that, after the second salvo had been dropped, the German infantry was able to take the position without losses.

In most Russian bombing attacks the planes would fly over a troop-filled road at a right angle, so that some bombs would be fairly certain to hit the target. In flying along the course of a road it often happened that all the bombs fell so far to the sides of the road as to be completely ineffective.

353. Bomber attacks at night bore the stamp of nuisance raids. In nearly all instances they were flown by individual planes, and directed against targets located close to the front, such as billets, highway trafic, artillery positions, and other points occupied by troops. They were annoying, to be sure, but seldom caused major damage. In order to make it difficult for the night bombers to locate their targets, especially on moonlit nights, we smeared all of the whitewashed houses with mud and conducted all movements without lights. Installation of small Flak units at persistently attacked points sufficed to drive off the night planes immediately and for a rather long time, since their silhouettes in the moonlight made them easy targets. Heavy losses of planes resulted.

354. Night attacks directed against large installations, such as railheads, airfields, factories, cities, etc., lasted all night. They were carried out by a chain of individual aircraft following each other at short intervals. Flights to and from the target followed different routes. Whenever the Russians aimed at destroying extensive installations, they repeated their bombing raids for several consecutive nights. In the summer of 1944, for example, most of the city of Tilsit in East Prussia was destroyed in a long series of Soviet night attacks.

355. On dark nights, Russian aircraft used parachute flares resembling Christmas trees to mark the direction of the bomb run and the

target areas for the attacking bombers. Frequently, however, inhabited places thus bracketed by a rectangle of flares could still be evacuated before the arrival of the first bombers. In other cases, the wind blew the rectangles so far away before the bombers appeared that all the bombs fell into open fields and caused no damage.

The Russians used German searchlights and other guide lights as navigation aids, and for that reason never attacked them.

In the East, enemy <u>night fighters</u> seldom appeared and were of very minor importance.

356. A faulty sense of orientation in the air, or an inadequate knowledge of map reading, repeatedly caused Russian pilots <u>accidentally</u> to <u>land</u> behind the German lines. In January 1943, for instance, a Russian pilot accompanied by an engineer landed his repair-shop plane south of the Donets River. The engineer was supposed to repair a plane which had made a forced landing, and, despite perfect visibility, happened to stray across the clearly recognizable river which formed the front. Much more distressing to the Russians was the accidental landing in the German Buczacz bridgehead of a liaison plane with courier mail and an Armeeintendant (administrative official of an army) aboard. That incident took place shortly before the Russian summer offensive east of Lwow in 1944. The pilot was flying from Kolomea to Tarnopol, but landed at the halfway mark because the similarity of terrain and the brown uniforms of a Hungarian unit, which he mistook for Russians, had confused him.

357. The Russians repeatedly used <u>captured German planes</u>,

with the German insignia retained, for purposes of reconnaissance and for occasional special missions.

PARTISAN WARFARE

CONTENTS

	Page
Chapter One - PARTISAN COMBAT METHODS	180
Chapter Two - DEFENSE AGAINST PARTISAN ACTIVITY	186
I. Passive Antipartisan Measures	186
II. Active Antipartisan Measures	188
Chapter Three - ACTIVITIES OF OTHER BANDS IN THE EAST	192

Chapter One

PARTISAN COMBAT METHODS

358. Generally speaking, Russian partisan groups on the Eastern Front were formed early in 1942. At first they were mainly isolated bands of little strength, frequently dropped from aircraft, and operating in rear areas. During the summer of 1942, however, these bands were gradually combined into more closely knit groups, put under a unified command, and continuously reinforced. Accordingly, their operations markedly grew in scope and impact.

359. Partisan group activities seldom covered areas near the front, except when extensive, pathless forests favored their approach. In general, the partisan groups would maneuver in the rear areas of the armies, in woods and swamps next to highways and railroads. They avoided open territory and regions occupied by German troops, but kept the latter under surveillance.

360. To begin with, our troops had difficulty defending themselves against this type of warfare. Its effectiveness had been underestimated. Apart from the fact that, considering the vast areas, our forces were not numerous enough to combat the steadily expanding partisan groups, the front-line troops, who had been trained for orthodox warfare, all lacked experience in antipartisan warfare.

361. During large-scale enemy break-throughs, or German withdrawals, strong partisan groups frequently managed to co-ordinate

their operations with those of Soviet cavalry, ski units, infiltrated infantry, or paratroops. Substantial forces (usually several infantry and panzer divisions) had to be mustered in order to combat the enemy joint efforts. MS # T-36, Example 15, relates one of the most significant and sweeping operations of that type. Prior to large-scale enemy offensives, strong bands would often migrate to the areas that the enemy soon hoped to take. Such movements, therefore, gave some indication of enemy intentions. Prior to the beginning of the large-scale enemy offensive in East Galicia (July 1944), for example, numerous bands worked their way into the Carpathian Mountains southwest of Lwow, which were among the objectives of the enemy operations.

362. On the other hand, during each enemy withdrawal, as well as subsequent to battles of encirclement, innumerable soldiers cut off from their own forces, and sometimes entire combat units, made their way to the partisans and fought with them. In such instances, too, partisan activities developed into a serious threat.

363. During the winter, strong bands, well organized from a military standpoint and commanded by specially trained leaders, developed intense activity in the very extensive woodlands of the Eastern Front.

The bands were generally organized into **groupments** of from 3,000 to 5,000 men each. As long as the front remained static, these groupments would remain in a fixed location; they were quartered in winter-proofed camps, excellently constructed and heavily guarded. Smaller groups, varying greatly in strength, comprised at least 100 men. Attached to each groupment was a number of these smaller partisan groups. They branched out through the entire rear area and frequently were only in loose liaison with the groupment. They constantly changed their position, and therefore were difficult to locate in the vast rear area, which was only sparsely occupied by troops. They had contact men in all the larger villages of importance to them. Dispersed and cut-off Russian units gave them even tactical striking power. In 1941, for instance, in the area of Army Group Center, ten thousand men under General Kulik operated very skillfully and could not be cornered. Another example was the remnants of the 32d Kazak Division, whose destruction required the commitment of German front-line troops on 6 and 7 August 1941. In 1944, activities of partisans, reinforced by infiltrated troops, had reached such proportions west of the extremely swampy Narva River that the left wing of the northern front (III SS Panzer Corps) had to be pulled back in order to form a shorter and more easily guarded line.

364. Every camp of the larger partisan groups was secured on all sides--in some sections to a depth of several hundred meters--by thick underbrush, brier obstacles, or abatis and wire entanglements. All roads leading to the camp had been blocked or camouflaged, or detours had been built which led in another direction. Traffic to the camp was conducted on paths known only to the initiated. Sometimes these paths were protected by bodies of water, with crossings built twenty to thirty centimeters below water level, or by large stretches of swamp that could be crossed only on swamp skis. All movements of

strangers were carefully controlled by sentries stationed far from camp and disguised as peasants. Strangers were also kept under close surveillance by a network of spies active in all villages in the vicinity.

365. The camps were well supplied with <u>weapons, ammunition, explosives, and rations</u>. Only very reliable partisans were put in charge of these supplies.

The camps procured their food supplies by means of forced requisitions in nearby villages. Villages refusing food contributions were ruthlessly put to the torch by the partisans; the men were dragged into the woods, and the women and children dispersed. Supplies were also received by aircraft, which dropped the rations in the immediate vicinity of the camp when prearranged light or fire signals were displayed. The looting of vehicles during partisan raids likewise provided ammunition and small arms for the bands.

366. <u>Excellent camouflage</u> prevented any aerial observation of the camps. The shelters were allowed to be heated only at night, so that no smoke would disclose the existence of the camp during the day. The partisans succeeded in maintaining the secrecy of the camps for a long time by having small bands appear in remote villages and by disseminating false rumors concerning partisan movements. The mere suspicion of betrayal was sufficient cause for execution of the suspect. The same fate threatened the family of the condemned. These measures explain why all partisan operations were kept secret. Whoever joined a partisan group, voluntarily or involuntarily, could leave it only at

the risk of his life.

367. The partisans also had <u>signal communications</u> at their disposal. The larger partisan units received their directives via short-wave <u>radio</u>, so that they had up-to-date information about current military developments in their respective sectors. <u>Air couriers</u> were also used. There was a carefully camouflaged landing place for liaison airplanes in the immediate vicinity of almost every major camp.

368. Practically without exception partisan operations were carried out at night. Daytime raids seldom took place, and then only in areas in which no German troops were stationed for miles around. Raids of that type were usually confined to individual motor vehicles. A <u>major partisan operation</u>, with the demolition of a railroad bridge as its objective, would proceed as follows:

A long column of women and children would move along the right of way in the direction of the bridge. Presuming them to be refugees, our own sentry would take no action. When the head of the column had reached the bridge, heavy surprise fire was directed against the bridgehead from the end of the column. Machine guns, set up on the roadbed in the direction of the bridge, pinned down our guards. Under this fire cover, and by utilizing women and children in violation of international law, the partisans succeeded in installing powerful demolition charges, which they had all prepared, and in destroying the bridge.

369. Partisan operations generally covered mining of main highways, demolition of railroad tracks, mining of railroad beds and

arming the mines with push and pull igniters, surprise fire attacks on trains, looting of derailed railroad cars, raids on trucks and convoys, and burning of ration, ammunition, and fuel depots. Less frequent were raids on command posts of higher headquarters.

370. The partisans followed the practice of avoiding open combat as much as possible. This practice was indeed the guiding rule upon which their method of warfare was based. Unusual developments at the front would immediately result in extremely lively partisan activity, essentially aimed at the disruption and destruction of railroad lines. During one of our major attacks, for instance, the main line of a railroad that had to handle the supplies for three armies was blasted at two thousand points in a single night and so effectively disrupted that all traffic was stalled for several days. Such large-scale operations at times seriously hampered the supply of our troops. They were carried out by small partisan teams and numerous individuals.

Chapter Two

DEFENSE AGAINST PARTISAN ACTIVITY

I. <u>Passive Antipartisan Measures</u>

371. <u>Creation of a special staff</u> whose duty it was to collect all information concerning the appearance and movement of partisans by means of close contact with the military authorities in the rear areas and with the Russian community heads, as well as by means of a network of agents in areas threatened by partisans. All information thus gathered would immediately be passed on to the military authorities concerned.

372. <u>Combining of small headquarters</u> in order to protect them more effectively against partisan raids.

373. <u>Formation of local defense units</u> in threatened areas, drawn from among the Russian population which had urgently requested this measure because it suffered very much from confiscation of cattle, forceful removal of men, etc., by the partisans.

374. <u>Halt of all traffic on especially endangered roads</u> at nightfall; use of such roads in daytime only at certain hours and in convoys escorted by armed guards.

375. Protection of railroads, bridges, and trains. Outguards within sight or earshot of each other were posted along railroad lines in threatened areas. The outguards were quartered in blockhouses protected by wire entanglements and abatis, behind which lay

also the entrenchments for defense. Wherever the railroad line led through wooded terrain, all trees within fifty meters of either side of the right of way were felled in order to provide a better field of vision.

376. Reinforced outguards equipped with infantry heavy weapons protected all **bridges**. Another precaution, however, had to be taken in addition to furnishing local protection for bridges and adjacent bridgeheads, particularly whenever larger bridges were to be safeguarded. Strong guard detachments had to be posted at a great enough distance to permit them to spot approaching partisan bands, and to allow time for an orderly preparation of countermeasures. Precautions of that nature had not been taken prior to the previously mentioned partisan operation against the railroad bridge.

377. All **trains** going through danger zones had two sand-filled gondola cars coupled to the front of their locomotives in order to protect the latter. Each train was escorted by a guard detachment of about forty men.

378. Furlough trains were guarded by the soldier-passengers themselves. For that reason, all men going on furlough had to carry their small arms (see MS # T-21). Night traffic on particularly imperiled railroad lines was discontinued from time to time. During the day, the trains on these lines sometimes traveled within sight of each other. This procedure, however, was possible only because Russian air activity in the rear area was very limited.

II. Active Antipartisan Measures

379. *Fighting the partisan bands*, a mission assigned primarily to units permanently designated for the purpose, such as security divisions and forces particularly organized for that purpose. The great depth of area required a substantial number of such units. Since they were not available in desired numbers, security divisions frequently had to be assigned zones that they were hardly able to control. In the forest terrain of Varanovichi and Minsk, for instance, the 707th Security Division had to guard an area of ninety thousand square kilometers (larger than all of Austria). Its duties usually consisted of the following:

Protection of important points in seriously threatened wooded areas. Surveillance and protection of zones and villages through which led military supply routes, and which were constantly imperiled by partisan bands; reconnaissance of partisan camps, and roads leading to them; daily dispatch of as many combat patrols as possible into partisan territory in order to prevent the partisans from uniting into groups and establishing permanent bases; operations against detected partisan camps.

380. If a major operation is planned against a detected partisan camp, it is of vital importance that the project be kept a strict secret from the troops. Experience has taught that if such plans are revealed, even larger partisan groups immediately dissolve, only to assemble again at a different location. It happened repeatedly that in carefully prepared operations, partisan camps, which shortly before had been fully occupied, were found deserted. The troops, therefore, must

be informed of the actual plans only after they have reached the outer line of encirclement.

381. The <u>assembly</u> of the attacking troops must take place at least one day's march away from the partisan camps. The advance toward the outer line of encirclement must be so timed that all troops will reach it simultaneously and occupy it immediately. As far as possible, the outer line of encirclement should be anchored on natural obstacles that are easy to block and keep under surveillance (e.g., rivers). The troops are to be deployed in the outer line of encirclement in such a manner that they will form a continuous line of sentries, with each soldier within calling distance—and at night, within sight—of the next. Behind this line of sentries, pursuit detachments are to be kept ready for immediate employment against partisan bands which might break out. As soon as the encirclement has been completed, leaflets are to be dropped over all inhabited places within the ring, ordering all inhabitants to evacuate at once and to assemble at a designated point.

382. The <u>contraction of the ring of encirclement</u> will proceed during daytime only, in phases covering not more than three to four kilometers per day, and the territory must be carefully combed. The sectors to be taken must have been occupied by at least two hours before twilight, so that the troops will be able to establish themselves and become acquainted with the terrain ahead while it is still light.

383. Sectors easily distinguishable in the woods (glades, paths, railroad lines) are to be designated as the new line of encir-

clement. Close contact between individuals must be maintained. Nighttime security at the sector boundaries is of particular importance. The procedure of detailing forces for guarding unit boundaries, as well as the command over those forces, must be clearly regulated. The further contraction of the ring up to the final encirclement of the camp follows the same pattern as described above.

384. As soon as the encirclement has started, the surrounded area must be kept under constant aerial observation. By means of dropping messages, the planes must immediately notify troops and officers in command of any observed break-out attempts. Since breakouts are to be expected mainly at night, sufficient security detachments must be posted in front of the sentry line. With the contraction of the ring of encirclement a proportionate number of reserves are to be withdrawn, and their follow-up must be properly regulated. If the partisans still remain in their camp by the time the troops have reached the final line of encirclement, a heavy air attack will usually enable the troops to score a quick success.

385. Experience has taught that this type of antipartisan warfare, though requiring large numbers of troops and much time, promises the greatest success. No other methods proved themselves in wooded terrain, since break-outs at night could hardly be prevented. Rigid discipline is a prerequisite for the success of an operation. The designated objective for the day may not be changed during the operation. Independent changes on the part of the troops disrupt the line of encirclement and make the break-out of partisans possible.

386. Winter proved to be the most favorable season for carrying out antipartisan operations, because all movements could be more readily observed in snow-covered terrain. In summer the dense foliage of the woods made the carrying out of such operations very difficult. The operations should, as far as possible, be carried out during bright nights, best of all during a full moon. As liberal as possible an armament with machine pistols proved advantageous. Mortars have more of a demoralizing than actual effect, since their shells burst in the trees. Artillery can hardly be used during advances in woods. It can usually be put into action only during the battle for the fortified camp itself. Depending upon the terrain, it may be advisable to have individual guns follow directly behind the leading elements. The employment of tanks, where the terrain is suitable, produces excellent results. In such operations the troops must have an adequate supply of signal pistols and cartridges. In the case of swampland, the troops must be equipped with swamp skis.

387. The wooded terrain, affording poor visibility, and deceptions at night often caused shooting frays that started a panic or resulted in firing on our own troops. It is therefore advisable to prohibit the firing of all infantry light weapons except during partisan attacks. Special regulations for opening fire also are required when the final ring of encirclement has been closed, and the troops are facing each other at a short distance.

Chapter Three

ACTIVITIES OF OTHER BANDS IN THE EAST

388. In addition to the Russian partisan groups, there also existed in the East strong Ukrainian and Polish groups, as well as a few weak Czech and Jewish groups. The latter two were of no great importance. Some of the bands were for, and others against Russia. They fought each other cruelly and ruthlessly to the point of annihilation. In 1944, for instance, at the Polish-Ukrainian linguistic frontier, Polish bands raided Ukrainian villages, and Ukrainian bands Polish villages, burned them, and massacred the entire population including women and children. There were insufficient German troops to occupy the entire territory densely enough to prevent such raids. Emergency detachments usually came too late.

389. Even behind the German front, severe fighting, even to the extent of employing heavy weapons, frequently broke out between the partisan groups of different camps. Such disturbances at times caused a local paralysis of Soviet partisan activity.

390. The very active bands of the Ukrainian Nationalist Movement (UPA) formed the strongest partisan group in the East next to the Russian Communist bands, and fought them bitterly. The UPA repeatedly offered its co-operation against the Soviet partisan bands to the German Army, and requested a German general to act as organizer and tactical leader. But the top leadership of the German Army, very much

to its disadvantage, continually refused these requests. Only tacit, local agreements were therefore made between the UPA and German military authorities. They proved advantageous to both parties. Sometimes the UPA would participate in fighting the Soviet Lands even without any previous agreement (in 1944 north of Lwow and at Stanislav). The UPA forces were deployed in groups of several thousands each in the rear of the Russian as well as the German armies. Although they fought the German political organizations and their police forces, they never fought the German troops, and they did seriously harass the Soviet Army. Not only did they severely impede its supply, they also attacked Russian headquarters and rendered them powerless by encirclement (for example, in 1944 a Russian corps headquarters in Korosten, which had to be liberated by motorized troops). Furthermore, they incited revolts of the Ukrainian population in the rear area (in Kiev, for example), the quelling of which required the withdrawal of several divisions from the front for an extended period of time.

391. Hostile bands can most effectively be checked by other bands. Such a modus operandi, however, is possible only in a country in which the people, or at least part of the people, join one's own troops. That prerequisite was met in the East (Ukraine, Don region, White Russia, and the Baltic States), but very little advantage was taken of it. Especially the Ukrainian movement, which was backed by forty million people, did not receive sufficient consideration.

392. Although seriously disturbing German supply operations, and thereby also the conduct of battle, even the strongest partisan move-

ment, that of the Soviets, had no decisive influence on the over-all operations in the East.

Ex. 38   Protection of Supply Lines near Kirovograd against Partisan Raids (1942-43)

393. The Kirovograd region was administered by civilian authorities with the aid of municipal and regional commissars, who had their seats in the larger towns. The former town and community boundaries were retained as much as possible. The security of the region was the responsibility of the regional military government officer (Feldkommandant) and the local military government officers (Ortskommandant) under him. It included mainly the security of railroads, the two important supply routes—express highways IV and IVc—as well as the Bug bridges at Pervomaisk and Voznesensk. Two local defense (Landesschuetzen) battalions were available for those tasks.

394. Except for occasional minor sabotage acts against railroads, telephone lines, etc., by the native population, the area administered by Regional Military Government Office (Feldkommandantur) 509 remained absolutely undisturbed throughout 1942, so that substantial progress could be made in the work on express highways IV and IVc. Not until March of 1943 did a sizable partisan group invade this area.

395. Of the railroad lines in this region, the one with the branch line to Dnepropetrovsk and Krivoi Rog, via Aleksandriya—Pyatikhatka, was the most vital from the military as well as the war-economy standpoint. The important junction and marshalling center of Znemenka was the point most vulnerable to sabotage operations. Had that place been destroyed, the entire supply of the front, and shipments of badly needed war materials destined for Germany, would have become seriously endangered for a rather long period of time.

396. The terrain was level and flat, with little vegetation. It was partially steppe land. Except for a fairly large, dense patch of forest between Znemenka and Tsibulnos, only smaller strips of woodland limited the visibility along the railroad line. Features extremely favorable for sabotage operations were the extensive

fields of sunflowers, growing taller than a man, and also, to a lesser degree, the grain fields.

397. Raids on the railroad line were always carried out in insidiously cunning ways by bands which found refuge mainly in the woods north of Znemenka and were willingly aided by elements among the population of the neighboring villages. Organized into small combat patrols (Troikas), and carefully protecting their lines of withdrawal, they blew up railroad tracks, damaged control towers and signal installations, and terrorized the native railroad personnel. The Troikas disappeared again upon the completion of their work of destruction, as a rule without having suffered any losses. Their activities were directed from a higher level, and they were regularly supplied with weapons, communications equipment, explosives, maps, medical supplies, etc., which sometimes were dropped by aircraft. The explosives consisted of demolition charges, mines, artillery shells, or improvised infernal machines.

The weapons of the Troikas were generally machine pistols, daggers, and rifles. The members wore civilian clothes, but some were dressed in uniforms of the German Army, Luftwaffe, or political organizations.

398. In March 1943, a partisan group, at first numbering from two hundred to three hundred men, with a few women as medical and signal personnel, invaded the region of Feldkommandantur 509 at Chigirin (54 kilometers west of Kremenchug). It was very ably led, and highly mobile in its conduct of battle. The group used sleighs in the winter, and requisitioned horses during the muddy period. For three weeks they roamed through this region; raided agricultural centers, sawmills, and other plants; killed the managers (Stuetzpunktleiter) of the agricultural centers as well as the superintendents (Landwirtschaftsfuehrer); liberated prisoners of war; and disrupted rail traffic at Sosnovka. The partisans sought shelter in villages adjacent to woodlands. Horses and vehicles were sheltered in steep ravines in order to protect them against artillery fire. The expertly arranged security and reconnaissance measures precluded the possibility of surprise raids by German troops. Orders and instructions were received via short-wave equipment which was kept in a suitcase. Because of their well-functioning intelligence machinery, searches of woodlands and villages for the smaller sabotage teams of

partisans were almost never successful. The Ukrainian community authorities' lists of inhabitants were seldom in order, and so the identification of the inhabitants of a village was very difficult. It was, therefore, found practicable to chalk the names of the residents of each house on the front door.

399. Focal points of security were railroad stations, control towers, wooded zones, and bridges. Shifting of reserves by motor vehicle was planned for a quick reinforcement of the defenses. All points that had to be defended were converted into strong points. Arrangements had to be made in buildings to permit firing from various floors, and machine-gun emplacements with flanking and alternate firing positions had to be installed. Plank walls had to be erected for protection against fragmentation, and windows had to be provided with gun shields and embrasures. Fire steps, ammunition lockers, communication corridors, and observation posts had to be established. Telephone lines were laid so as to be protected as much as possible against gun fire, and supplemented by optic and acoustic alarm signals.

In the vicinity of each strong point, the terrain was cleared of obstructing vegetation for a distance of about one kilometer in each direction along the railroad line; this cleared area extended some three hundred to four hundred meters from the tracks.

400. The goal of the <u>conduct of operations</u> was to assure the smooth functioning of rail traffic. In addition to military security, the railroad lines were frequently inspected by employees walking along the tracks, and patrolled by means of handcars, or locomotives pushing freight cars ahead of them. The speedy formation of "alert" units for fire fighting, and the procedure of transporting them by motor or rail had to be planned and practiced in drills. The use of armored trains, or the addition to trains of cars carrying troops, proved to be effective methods of antipartisan defense.

401. <u>Experiences</u>

The military forces were not sufficient for the manifold tasks of railroad security. In order to ease their burden, local inhabitants were assigned to the troops as socalled <u>voice-alarm sentries</u>. Upon spotting partisans, these sentries were to shout the information to their neighboring guard posts, stationed at a distance of five hundred meters, but were not to fight. For that reason they were unarmed. Their reliability varied, since they feared the cruel reprisals of the partisans against themselves and their families. The <u>indigenous forces</u>, some of which were employed for railroad defense, likewise functioned only when they were heavily intermixed with German units. The Landesschuetzen units were not properly armed. Their equipment, too, was completely inadequate. For reconnaissance, the Fieseler-Storch (liaison aircraft) proved equal to all demands. The evacuation of villages directly adjacent to railroad lines, and the establishment of so-called death zones, within which any civilian would be shot on sight, were found to be appropriate measures.

CONCLUSIONS

402. The success of any armed force flows from a sum total of measures not only in the military field, but also in the spheres of politics, national indoctrination, economics, and others, which in their entirety decide the outcome of a war. They all must therefore be analyzed and weighed against each other if one would find the ultimate causes of victory or defeat. Only the product of intensive studies would form a positive basis for the evaluation of an armed force in a past war, and thereby offer also clues as to its potential in a possible future conflict.

In the preceding pages, none but the military phase—and it is important—could be taken under scrutiny. The present study in itself, however, throws light on many significant aspects that permit readily applicable conclusions to be drawn concerning this subject.

403. Not the success alone, but also the circumstances under which it was achieved form the standards by which an armed force is to be evaluated. The Red Army was successful in the last war, a good argument for the proposition that in a future war, fought under equal or similar conditions, it would again emerge victorious. The higher command was good, and in its hands, the troops, purely as a human mass, were a useful instrument. The prime motive force behind both was Communism; the final goal, World Revolution.

404. Manpower and materiel were abundant, and may be presumed to be abundant also in the future. The Soviets have a wealth of war experience on the basis of which to train their leaders and masses in up-to-date methods. They also have the means to maintain quantity

and quality of their equipment at a high level. Accordingly, one might think the final conclusion from this study and the description of climatic conditions in the East has to be, "Hands off Russia; the Russian combination of mass and space cannot be overpowered!"

405. That, however, is not the case. It should not be forgotten that much that might be said about Russia and the Russian has had to be condensed here as well as in MS # T-36. In that connection, the terrain difficulties and the characteristics of the Russian soldier have had to be described one after the other in such a way that both could easily be overestimated. Despite Russia and the Russian, despite cold and mud, despite inadequate equipment and a virtually ridiculous numerical inferiority, the German soldier actually had a victory over the Soviets within his grasp. The preceding accounts throw the magnitude of German achievements in the Eastern Campaign from 1941 to 1945 into bold relief.

406. Let the reader imagine, however, an army free from those deficiencies, not handicapped by having substantial forces tied up on other fronts, backed up by an adequate industrial potential; let him, on the other hand, imagine a Russia that receives no outside aid. Under such circumstances no expert will doubt a victory over the Soviet Union, even if the very latest tools of warfare are available to both parties.

407. The prerequisite, however, for a successful war against the U.S.S.R. is a <u>systematic preparation</u> for the undertaking. One cannot provoke such a conflict and expect to carry it through in a spirit

of adventure. The equipment of the soldiers, and the total amount of materiel must meet the requirements of the Russian countryside in all seasons. This is a question of industrial potential, which, by applying the experiences gathered in the last war, is not difficult to solve. Training, tactical as well as physical, must comply with the above-mentioned peculiarities of combat against the Russian and on Russian soil. Training aimed at imparting <u>toughness, independence</u>, and <u>willingness to assume responsibility</u>, and the molding of <u>self-reliant individual fighters</u>, as well as leaders who are willing to take chances, are the most essential points in this respect. <u>Strict</u> discipline is an additional fundamental condition for every one who fights in Russia. Even the best athletic background is insufficient to meet the severity of this test. And, last but not least, there must be <u>inner conviction</u> of the soldier, the indomitable will to prevent the Russian Moloch from seizing the world.

GERMAN REPORT SERIES

Previously Distributed:

(U)	<u>A</u> <u>G</u> <u>P</u> <u>G</u> (20 Sep 44 - 3 Dec 44) <u>REPORT OF THE CHIEF OF STAFF</u>	(A-999)
(C)	WARFARE IN THE FAR NORTH	(T-24)
(R)	AN AIRBORNE PANZER CORPS	(B-628)
(U)	<u>A</u> <u>G</u> <u>P</u> <u>B</u> (25 Jan 45 - 21 Mar 45) <u>REPORT OF THE CHIEF OF STAFF</u>	(A-964)
(C)	PECULIARITIES OF RUSSIAN WARFARE	(T-22)
(U)	<u>O</u> <u>B</u> <u>W</u> <u>E</u> <u>S</u> <u>T</u> (Atlantic Wall to Siegfried Line) <u>A</u> <u>STUDY</u> <u>IN</u> <u>COMMAND</u>	(B-308)
(C)	UNIFICATION OR COORDINATION --THE ARMED FORCES PROBLEM	(T-113)

www.ingramcontent.com/pod-product-compliance
Lightning Source LLC
Chambersburg PA
CBHW081834170426
43199CB00017B/2729